From Blue to Khaki

(Per ardua ad . . .
          . . Certa Cito)

S S *Eastern Prince*
Prince Line of Furness Withy & Co
11,000 tons

From Blue to Khaki

(Per ardua ad . . .
. . Certa Cito)

R. Harvey Blizard

The Pentland Press Limited
Edinburgh • Cambridge • Durham • USA

First published in 1996 by
The Pentland Press Ltd.
1 Hutton Close
South Church
Bishop Auckland
Durham

British Library Cataloguing in Publication Data.
A Catalogue record for this book is available
from the British Library.

ISBN 1 85821 423 8

Typeset by CBS, Felixstowe, Suffolk
Printed and bound by Antony Rowe Ltd., Chippenham

CONTENTS

Also by the same author

One Ear to the Ground
published by
Cannongate Books
Hythe
Kent
CT21 5PX

Chapter 1

INTO THE BLUE

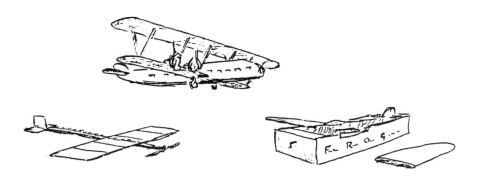

Time is the problem. This is nothing new, it has been with us for centuries. J.B. Priestly was intrigued by it in his Time plays, and Nanky Poo made fun of it. In my own case, I am convinced that I inherited it from my mother. She was not a time keeper, and she did not like day-light saving. She preferred to shut out the cold winter evenings by drawing the curtains, and her most hated day in the calendar was in March when the clocks moved forward one hour. For two or three years in middle-age, she decided that she would put up with it no longer. All the other clocks in the house were allowed to change, but not her kitchen clock. It remained on GMT. Thereafter, for about a week, she waged war on the rest of the world, remaining on her own timetable. Living in the depths of the country, in Dorset, her defences remained intact until she turned on the wireless – as it was known in those days – when a soliloquy would occur in which she described in lurid detail exactly what she thought of the whole business.

As I have said, I am sure my own problem stems from her. My particular time-warp being that I have progressed through life for over seventy years, with only sixty of them used up. I am not sure where I lost the odd ten; it must have been very early on, because my maturity has always been this amount younger than all my compatriots. I passed my exams, and I think I looked alright, but at the age of eighteen I was a naive twelve year-old, and at thirty I was just approaching twenty-one. This was a disadvantage at the time, but now that I have graduated to becoming an elderly gentleman, it is a huge bonus to find that my physical and mental output can equal, if not better, many men my junior by a decade.

This is the background to my Erk's progress. An Erk, you will recall, was the lowest form of animal life in the RAF. A creature in blue with nothing on his arm except the RAF eagle; not even the propeller of an LAC (Leading Aircraftsman). To his fellow Erks, he was affectionately known as an AC Plonk.

Jingoism and martial arts were not my middle names. However, there was a war on and, at the age of eighteen, I had to do my bit. A choice had to be made.

Light blue, dark blue or khaki?

Khaki. I was brought up under excessive discipline, and excessive discipline can produce a 'bolshie bastard'. He does not have to be the aggressive sort; he can be scheming and underhand, achieving his aim through subterfuge. Such a one is RHB. Stepfather had never made any bones about it – the army – but my contrariwise nature said 'not on your nelly'.

Dark blue. I had no feeling for the sea. Meeting some very large waves when I was eight dampened any enthusiasm I might have had!

Which left light blue. There was something about aeroplanes which appealed more than boats and tanks.

My aeronautical interest had been kindled early in life when one of the huge Imperial Airways machines flew over our house – I wonder why? What an impressive monster. A huge biplane, painted silver, with portholes in the fuselage to allow the passengers a sight of the world at their feet; and its four engines mounted between the upper and lower wings. This was something for a boy to think about.

Quite early in life I had been given a contraption which was in vogue at the time. It consisted of a wooden framed wing about three feet by four inches, covered in silk. This was attached to a 'fuselage' made of a single thin square piece of wood about two feet long. A tail plane was at the back, and a propeller at the front. Elastic was the motor power. One wound the propeller anti-clockwise to charge the machine, then held the whole thing aloft and, theoretically, it flew. As often as not, it didn't, and occasionally over enthusiastic winding of the elastic would result in a loud snap and torn silk. I failed to qualify as a pilot!

Another aeronautical experience was in 1931 when one of my aunts took me to Southampton to see the Schneider trophy. Crowds of us sat along the shore and watched the Supermarine Spitfire go through its paces. To nineteen thirties' eyes it seemed to dash across the sky at lightning speed, though in fact it was chugging along at only 340 mph. There was no proper race that year for a reason I cannot remember, but the speed constituted a record for the 'race' to date.

Frog. FROG. To you, my reader, this probably means a small leaping animal found near a pond. Alternatively, a potentially gastronomic meal at a French restaurant. But you would be wrong. It stands for 'Flies Right Off Ground'. I go back to the nineteen thirties when this particular frog was served up in a little cardboard box measuring approximately 12" x 4" x 3". It had a picture of an aeroplane on the outside, dressed in more or less Spitfire guise. One removed the lid and there was a small fuselage lying in the box, complete with tail plane at one end and propeller at the other. Two wings were lying alongside. The box had two cutaway pieces where the wings fitted, so one attached them to the fuselage while in the box. Then one did something at the front end where there was a winding mechanism, and hey-presto, the machine was ready to 'fly right off ground'.

Mecca, to a small boy at that time living in Guildford, was a toy shop in Swann Lane in a pedestrian fareway. My daily trip to the Grammar School (one term only) at the top of the town was up the length of the High Street. When time permitted I diverted to window-gaze at Mecca. I tried to will the Frog into my possession. Memory tells me that it cost 7/ 6, but perhaps it was not as much as that when one considers that Mr Ford was selling an all functioning motor car for £100. I was eventually given a Frog.

In the mid thirties, Sir Alan Cobham visited Crewkerne (our nearest town) with his Airshow. The site was somewhere down by the station, a mile out of town. I was taken to this jamboree and goggled at these contraptions of canvas and wire. I was allowed to go up for a 10/- (or was it 5/-?) flight. My mother subjected the pilot to a short discourse before take-off, on the care he was to take of her 'precious bundle'. I shuffled about with embarrassment, but was eventually allowed to clamber into the passenger's seat, and then treated to my ten-minute view of Crewkerne from 1,000 feet. It was a pity that we did not venture six miles to the south so that I could see our house from the air, but we didn't, and I was quite satisfied with what I had seen.

The thirties was a decade of fabulous names to my generation; Amy Johnson (Mollison) and husband Jim, Campbell, Seagrave, Lindenberg, Erhart and other pioneers. These were the heroes of youth, and models of their machines were play-things. What a gulf existed between my stepfather, in his sixties, and myself. His world was horses, and he had little time for all these new-fangled machines. To me, the modern world was brought to life at the cinema through the newsreels when I saw Amy

Johnson stepping out of her primitive plane.

Having, I hope, established a reasonable case for my choice of the RAF, it would be dishonest to overlook the attraction of the colour itself. Airforce blue was a nice colour and the thought of dressing up in it was far more appealing than either dark blue or khaki.

I hope my reader will now bear with me if I divert briefly from the main flight path. The subject is still aeroplanes but the context is different. Let us call it a flight of fancy.

Sir Alan Cobham. He has cropped up again recently when I read Nevil Shute's *Sliderule*. Readers of my earlier book *One Ear to the Ground* will know that I have a particular weakness for Nevil Shute. *Sliderule* is his autobiography, and to my delight I found that quite a few aspects of its content impinged upon my own RAF experience. Sir Alan was closely involved with Mr Norway (Shute's own name) when he set up his aircraft company in 1930, and the ultimate outcome of this development was production of the Airspeed Oxford, used by the RAF as a training machine. During my time in the RAF, I encountered this machine, thus I feel that I have an indirect contact with the great man himself. The Airspeed Oxford had a most distinctive sound.

Of equal interest was Shute's discourse on the R100 and R101. He was very involved with the development of the former, and even though it was built near York, it flew down to Cardington and was housed in one of the two huge hangars there. As readers will discover in Chapter Three, it was to Cardington that we were posted for our basic training, and we performed some of that training in those very hangars – which are still standing. Shute's tale of the development of those two airships is as alarming as any modern débâcle. What a tale of incompetence as far as the government-backed R101 was concerned; its fatal crash was almost a foregone conclusion. Adding spice to this chronicle, I have a distant relative, now in his late eighties, who was involved in pioneering work. In 1930, when a student for City and Guilds, he attended a lecture given by the Royal Autonautical Society. The subject was 'Strength of materials', and he remembers the lecturer tearing the design of the R101 to pieces, pointing out that the safety factor of some components was less than 2 to 1. How right he was, but it leaves one with little faith in government projects.

I have copies of two letters in my possession which are reproduced at Appendix A and B. They have nothing to do with the immediate subject in hand, but one was written by the father of my above-named relative and throws an interesting light on the attitude of Germany's young men toward Britain before the First World War. The other is self-explanatory. It was written by a young man to his parents following the death of his elder brother in 1917. He himself was killed in the forthcoming attack he refers to.

Chapter 2

HEADS OR TAILS

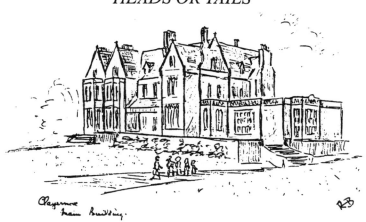

Clayesmore
from Building.

Toss a coin. Heads or tails? Such is life, where is one's destiny?

An AC Plonk. Was this what a public school education was designed
to produce? Surely not; but everyone has to start somewhere, so why not
at the bottom of the RAF ladder?

According to theory, public schools are intended to produce leaders;
plenty of self-confidence, with a good education to back it up. Clayesmore
did not lack in this respect; it was one of the smaller public schools, with
an almost avante-garde outlook for the times. We were right out in the
country, in Dorset, and we were exposed to an outdoor life. Our uniform
was open-necked shirts and shorts, which was unusual for the thirties.
We donned collars and ties only on Sundays. There was no school in the
afternoons; boys took part in games twice a week, hobbies twice a week
and manual labour on the fifth afternoon. The school stood in well over a
hundred acres of ground, and such land required husbandry. It was the

7

school policy that the boys should contribute their share, and so, once a week, every boy turned out in overalls, as appropriate, and was detailed off to some job requiring attention. This ranged from rolling the cricket pitch to repairing fences, to the supreme achievement – the building of an outdoor, full size, swimming pool. Many, many, cubic yards of earth were shifted in this enterprise, and I arrived at the school in 1936 as it was being finished. It was a proud achievement for the school to be able to state in the prospectus that the boys had built their own swimming pool. It was of course, unheated, so the sting in the tail – or perhaps more correctly, cold reality – was that every morning, in the summer term, all Houses had to troop down to the pool before breakfast, line up on the side, strip off, and do two widths.

Clayesmore has celebrated its centenary in 1996, and it is interesting to observe that all the above attributes date back to its founder, Alexander Devine (Lex). He was a revolutionary of his time and took boys who could not settle at other schools, from Eton downwards. He harnessed them and they thought the world of him. In particular, he believed in a broadest possible education embracing academic learning, sport, all the arts and accomplishments. He believed in hard physical work. From whatever station in life, he believed a boy should be able to wield a pick axe and shovel. From this his 'Manual' was born, and perpetuated. I joined the school in 1936, and my Headmaster was Evelyn M. King. He had been brought onto the staff by Lex in 1930 when aged only 22 in the belief that he would carry on Lex's traditions. He did, and became Headmaster in 1935.

Memories. Morning roll call. Attwood, Ballantyne, Ball major, Ball minor, Blizard, Burrell.

For hobbies afternoons we could choose anything we liked and the facilities included most of the things you could think of – art, book-binding, sculpture, printing, woodwork etc. etc.

8

In addition to these afternoon hobbies, there were numerous clubs which met in the evenings. These embraced such things as photography, play-reading, and debating to name but a few. No boy could leave that school without an interest having been kindled in some sort of interest in the wider aspects of education. I have no doubt at all that the foundation of most of my later life's interests were established at Clayesmore. Not least of these was music, prompted entirely by my house-master – JDS. On Sunday mornings one silent hour was devoted to writing home. This was part of the school programme, and applied to all. Needless to say, most boys had scribbled their page of non-news to parents by the end of half an hour, so the second half tended to develop into disorder. Our house-master said, 'Enough of this, we will have music.' Thereafter, at 12.30, he would appear in the common room with portable gramophone and a few 78s. He would then expound for a few minutes on *Eine Kleine Nachtmusik*, Mozart's 39th symphony, The Flying Dutchman overture, or whatever, followed by his playing the records. Speaking personally, I lapped it up, and that half hour was the highlight of the week. His inspiration was such that I wanted a gramophone of my own, and my mother managed to obtain an old one from my godfather. This served me for some time, however it was not as good as it might have been, so the squirrel habit set in, and I eventually accumulated enough half crowns to buy a five guinea Columbia model from a discount service (Colonel Keen) for four guineas. It was slightly strange to see the boy arriving at school at the beginning of term, complete with gramophone and case of records; however, it seemed to be accepted, and there were times when I gained a few minutes of popularity from my possession. Quite often I played my gramophone in the empty class room at week-ends and I remember one particular occasion when JDS heard my Deanna Durbin record of the drinking song from *La Traviata*. The door suddenly burst open, and he wanted to know who was doing what. He gave me further encouragement.

This was not the end of his influence. He taught history, and he had the ability to bring the pages to life. He was not content with the set manuals; he would seek out volumes on the periods we were studying, then read extracts to encourage us to read them ourselves. 'Royal Flush', 'The Proud Servant' when we were doing the Stuarts; 'Cardinal Ximines' when we were reading the Golden Age of Spain, and so on. He was a first-class teacher and could put any subject over to me.

Unfortunately, of course, where there is good, there is also a bad. JDS did not teach all subjects. CV taught us chemistry. A double period on Wednesdays. I loathed it as much as I enjoyed the Sunday morning music lessons. Chemistry was not my natural subject, the formulae were little more than letters selected at random from the alphabet, with the odd digit attached to them. Bottles of solutions were a mystery to me, and the effect of mixing any two together was beyond comprehension. CV registered the state of Blizard's mind on his pet subject from the outset, so any hope of a rapport between us was quickly dispelled. I became an early version of Shirley Valentine. Just occasionally, I might come out with the equivalent of 'wheels', but the frequency was so rare that it did not count. I was the duffer of the class, indeed of the whole school. I might have coped with this, and acclaimed such distinction with pride, but the final blow to me was CV's sarcasm. It folded me up. We made indelible impressions on each other, and I remember reading in the school magazine, some years after I had departed, a scathing reference to Blizard's chemistry ability. Having said all this, you may be surprised to know that I gained a pass in the subject, in my school certificate! This was due to the fact that CV had a knack of forecasting the questions we would be asked. The recipe worked in 1939. I answered like a parrot.

I feel very strongly about teaching. My grandfather was a headmaster, and my two aunts were school mistresses. At prep-school, history was my dismal subject, whereas later, at Clayesmore, it became my favourite. Why? Because of the teacher. I was an instructor in the army for two years during the fifties. I attended a method of instruction course, and so learned the techniques. Without undue self-congratulation, I know that I am a fairly good instructor. Against this I would say that I am not particularly well qualified in any subject, which brings me to the point. A teacher requires an adequate knowledge of his subject but it does not have to be to degree standard. My experience has been that the best instructors are those most able to put their subjects across to their trainees, in spite of, rather than because of, their academic qualification. Letters after one's name do not make for a better teacher; in fact, it is often the opposite. When I was at OCTU (Officer Cadet Training Unit) in India, radio theory was taught by two officers. Both were well qualified, but one more so than the other. Do I need to go on? The highly qualified officer rambled on and we had little idea of what he was talking about, while the lesser qualified gentleman had the knack of making the subject both interesting and intelligible. If he failed to put some point of theory across first time round, he would go through it again using a different approach, and most people then got it.

As an instructor one can tell straight away whether or not one is in tune with the class. If not, one can talk for forty-five minutes and it will be wasted hot air. When this happens, it is far better to stop in one's tracks, tell a funny story to get them listening, then start again.

The same argument applies to parents as much as teachers. See the problem through the child's eye. In this respect, I have been more than lucky; my wife seems to know exactly how a child thinks, and is therefore able to put her message across to them. If only parents (and teachers) could put themselves in the child's place, then I am sure we would be able to produce a generation of ideal citizens. The majority of grown-ups seem to have forgotten completely what it was like to be a child; they can only see the world from their own blinkered viewpoint. My stepfather definitely fell into this category. He had absolutely no idea of how obstacles, which were insignificant to him, were gigantic to a small boy. During the summer, we made regular expeditions down to the coast, to a place called Ypres near West Bay. I cannot say that I enjoyed these outings at the best of times, but one particular occasion sticks in my mind. There was a wind blowing, with rollers coming in; no doubt they were quite small, but to me at the age of eight, they were huge. I think I had not yet learned to swim, but even if I had, I was not very confident. My stepfather took me into this raging cauldron, and I was petrified. If only he had been able to understand how that sea appeared to me.

At one stage in my army career, I attended a course on nuclear warfare. On return to station, I was required to give three lectures on the subject to my brother officers. At two o'clock on the selected day, I duly held forth. With such a dramatic story to tell, I had no difficulty in holding my audience spellbound. I revealed the effects of atomic blast, radiation, fall-out, rotogens and all the rest. Had anyone in that room let drop one small pin, its impact on the floor would have been as great as the bomb itself. I had them in my hand – with one exception. Officer Commanding station, who was rather elderly, sat in the middle of the front row, fast asleep. Fortunately he did not snore, but I was very tempted to throw my chalk at him, in traditional school-masterly fashion.

As I have said, looking back, I am able to appreciate fully the interests which Clayesmore gave me. I have much to thank the school for, though I was not aware of it at the time.

Additional to the things already mentioned, I would single out the material presence of the school building itself; a large handsome country mansion set in its own extensive grounds including a lake. From the moment I set eyes on the main building, it did something to me. I was not unfamiliar with large country houses in Dorset and Somerset. My mother and stepfather knew most of their owners, so that I had access to them. But Clayesmore was different, more majestic. It had been built in 1897 for the Second Lord Wolverton by the Victorian architect Alfred Waterhouse, and embraced a model village, also built by him to serve the estate. All the door handles in the house bore the 'W' monogram on oval-shaped knobs. There was a huge extension at one end of the building which had been built as a double billiard room. It was oak panelled, and divided internally so as to form two parts. The cavernous fireplaces were designed to burn tree trunks from the estate. It had a polished oak floor which led from a long wide mosaic floored hall. This was the library, and was my favourite place. I spent many hours there. Although having been slow to start reading, I subsequently developed the taste and by the time I arrived at Clayesmore, I was an avid reader. I devoured the plays of Bernard Shaw, James Barrie, and others, and travelled the world socially, geographically, and historically, through the written word.

One thing the school failed to teach me was leadership, though to be fair this was not their prime policy. They were more concerned with helping boys to find themselves. Therefore, at the age of seventeen I departed the school without a vestige of leadership quality. However, this was not altogether surprising since I arrived having had no practice in this art. I was not ready for the hurly burly of life among a lot of boisterous boys, senior in both age and maturity. I took the easiest course, and one which I was quite used to. I shut myself off. I made few friends and cannot think why I was not bullied and sat upon. I wasn't, because I suppose I merged into the background as a non-person. My mental attitude caused a 'hoo-ha' in 1937 when I entered a poem entitled 'Meditation' in a school competition:

13

When the first few glimmering streaks of dawn
Show as herald to the following morn,
I think of those who possess not a bed
And are forced to steal, that they may be fed.

When a gale is howling around my house,
And I lie in bed, snug as a mouse,
The world I forget in a joyful ride
As I slumber in sleep with dreams as my guide.

For tramping the roads the day has not come
Without any money this gauntlet to run,
To be quite alone in an unkind world
With very few clothes around me enfurled.

But when this wearisome period is past
Then may I arrive in glory at last,
And walk in the glow as the home light gleams
And once again shall I slumber in dreams.

Coming from such a young pen, I suppose it was not surprising that it created quite a stir in the hierarchy. In due course, my mother and stepfather were summoned to the headmaster's study to discuss it. I was not told of the outcome.

For the first eleven years of my life I had been brought up more or less alone so that there was nobody to lead – or indeed follow. My years at a very small prep. school had introduced me to a slightly more gregarious lifestyle, but I had not fully adjusted. Thus, when I found myself with over 100 boys, I cocooned myself off from them and went my own way, absorbed in myself, trying to shut out the world I now found myself inhabiting. This was a trait which I usefully continued to exploit when I found myself living in a barrack room as an Erk. Perhaps I should say that in later years, my wife has found the same habit exasperating on more than one occasion. (She accepts that, in old age, I have become rather deaf, but insists that my ears were never one hundred per cent operational.) Perhaps she is right, after all; my mind has never been short of things to think about, and much more interesting things than those of my immediate surroundings. I sometimes wish that my mind would take half an hour off for NAAFI break; for instance, the writing of this chapter has taken place at almost any minute of any hour of any twenty-four-hour period – in the bath, at breakfast, in the middle of the night, when gardening, when driving, during washing up – at all or any of these times. The wording of this very paragraph has come to me while painting the dining room door – white –; listening to Dvorak's fourth symphony. So what hope have I?

Being an only child, brought up by my mother and a stepfather twice her age, in the remote countryside, I was not accustomed to people of my own age. For a few years I had the companionship of the Blackdown House groom's son who lived just up the road, but apart from him, I did not meet other boys, or girls. Looking at the matter dispassionately, a small boy in this ménage was not an asset, particularly when funds were short. His education was to be a major problem. My stepfather had been at Downside, to be followed there by his own son John whom you will meet later, and who was the same age as my mother. I am sure my stepfather would have liked me to go there too, but I doubt if my mother would have agreed to a catholic establishment. However, funds would not run to it, nor indeed to any other fee-paying school. Thus for the first eleven years of my life I was educated at home. These years were devoted to the installation of discipline, self-discipline and self-sufficiency; things which were to become the hall-mark of my whole life. If I wanted something, I

15

had to work for it, or if I wanted to buy something which my parents did not consider necessary, then I had to make a contribution towards its cost. Not a bad doctrine: God helps those who help themselves, or conversely, easy come, easy go. My own children were brought up to the same principles with, I believe, no regrets on either side.

No matter what I was doing, when the clock read nine a.m., it was time to sit at my own workplace and do lessons; no one cleaned my shoes, but they had to be well polished, and nobody cleaned up after me. Thus, the small boy that eventually ventured to school found his values somewhat different from those of his companions.

At last it was decided that some formal schooling could be avoided no longer. Two brief spells at Guildford (one term at the Grammar School) had not worked, mainly due to ill health, and so, as a result of grandfather and two aunts pooling resources, a place was found for me at a tiny prep. school at Coombe Florey, run by the rector. (This financial assistance, plus a bursarship, allowed me to continue my schooling at Clayesmore.) Three years at this establishment, and I was just beginning to find my feet amongst less than twenty other boys.

In the meantime, I learned one or two lessons which are worth recounting. The most lasting memory, and of great significance to the conduct of my life thereafter, was a broken promise. At some stage during my sojourn at the school, the headmaster's daughter decided that she would take a small party of boys to Taunton to see the film *King Kong*. I was not in the party, but she said that she would take all those of us who had missed out to another film later on during the term. It never happened, and I thought this very wrong. I was so offended that I vowed that if ever I said that I would do something specific for someone, then however casual the promise might be, I would honour it. I have done my best to keep this vow – in spite of the occasional forgetfulness – which shows how a tiny incident can shape a human character for life.

16

The whole school – family, boys and masters – sat down to meals together. The Dutton brothers were pupils at the school, and the younger one shared my somewhat unusual name of Harvey. I sat next to Edward at meal times. One day Edward and I disagreed on some subject we were discussing, and in exasperation, I told him, 'Shut up.' It happened to be a moment of silence at the dining table. No less than twenty-five pairs of eyes focused on me, Mr Rector, Mrs Rector, Mr and Mrs Rector's daughter, masters various, and all the boys.

'Who said that?' thundered the Rector. 'Never let me hear you say such a thing again.' How I longed for a cavernous hole to appear at my feet.

On another occasion, the nasty little boy enjoyed all the satisfaction of Jack Horner. We had been turned loose in Woolworths in Taunton. At the next meal, the Rector enquired of each boy what he had bought, whereupon, he gave judgement. When my turn came, I said I had bought R.D. Blackmore's *Lorna Doone*. Praise reached the rafters. 'All you other boys, note the example which has been set by Blizard.' My moment of glory. No doubt some other boy had bought *No Orchids for Miss Blandish* but wisely kept quiet about it.

Nostalgia. Two popular songs of the time: 'Red sails in the sunset' and 'The Isle of Capri'.

On a day in the summer of 1936, my stepfather came to discuss my future with the Rector. They parted company at about four o'clock. Within half an hour, the rector had died of a heart attack. I was incredulous. 'But I saw them shake hands only half an hour ago.' Such is life – or death.

Not infrequently, in adult life, one finds one's loyalties divided. I experienced this at the age of fourteen. You will recall that, in 1936, the country experienced the convulsions of the abdication of King Edward VIII. There were strong currents running through society at the time. My stepfather, a retired Indian Army colonel, with a DSO decoration, was a staunch Edward supporter. Had Edward announced a call to arms, the colonel would have been the first to enroll. Thus it was that he declined to agree with George VI mounting the throne. He felt so strongly about it that he decided that he would no longer respect the playing of the National Anthem. At that time, the family attended the local cinema at Crewkerne once or even twice a week; his feelings manifested themselves when he, followed by my mother, with myself bringing up the rear, marched out of the circle either prior to or during the playing of the National Anthem. Needless to say, I supported this action.

At the beginning of the spring term in 1937, a play entitled *Hawk Island* was staged at Blandford, and a party of boys, including me, attended a performance. After the final curtain, the National Anthem was played, so Blizard, true to family tradition, picked up his cap and coat and walked out. During the following few hours, I was made fully aware of where my loyalties ought to rest. I did not do it again.

Omissions tell a tale, and my observant readers will have noticed an important omission so far. No reference has been made to sport. Sport is a prime character builder, and probably induces self-confidence more than any other single aspect of a child's upbringing. I have no doubt that this deficiency was more to blame for my immaturity than any other. In self-defence, however, I would say that if was not entirely my fault. A chicken and egg situation: one required a certain amount of built-in self-confidence to start on the road to greater self-confidence. Generally speaking, sport involves a ball, and up to the age of eleven I had hardly met one. Most children kick these things around from the time when they first find their feet. They grow up with them, and a ball is the main source of entertainment when two or three boys are gathered together. As I have already said, I did not have the company of other boys, and a sixty-year-old stepfather did not indulge in such pastimes. True enough, I did not need this entertainment; I was in the country, and took myself off for walks by myself, or with the dogs. There was so much to see and watch all around me, that I had no need of these man-made spheres. I had access to other people's horses and ponies. I was planted on ponies from the age of six onwards. I am told that I was a very competent rider; I took part in gymkhanas and followed hounds. I was blooded at my first kill when I was so young that I can only vaguely remember it. My stepfather, with great pride, would tell his friends that Harvey always turned up at the end of a run – he didn't know how I got there, but I did. My mount was a rotund Shetland pony called 'Tar Baby'. We were friends. 'Muleface' was a larger and appropriately named beast and one day he bolted across a field towards the gate. I hung on, but the gate was closed so Muleface did a swift right turn. I continued 'Toujour a droit', landing cheek by jowl against the stone wall supporting the gate post. I arrived home with a fragile face and dented dignity. We were not friends. The funny thing is that I never looked upon myself as a good horseman, and quite apart from the expense, I have had no urge to continue riding into adult life. I also spent many days out on shoots, so, to be truthful, I arrived at school as a sportsman, but the wrong sort in that company. Perhaps it was the worst of both worlds – I was an ignoramus at the one, and could not display my prowess at the other. You may wonder why I did not find some ability at my prep. school. The answer was that there were so few boys that there were not enough of us to make two teams. Cricket and football did not play a large part in the curriculum. Everyone else was better than me anyway, so that my first encounter with the real thing was at Clayesmore.

During the first week at Clayesmore, new boys were assessed on the playing field. It was obvious that I had no idea, so was relegated without further ado to the halt, maim, and blind number two squad. This was the no-hope contingent, and games afternoon for Number Two squad was a joke for the rest of the school. I think that perhaps, if I had been given some elementary tuition in what to do with a ball, I might have got the idea. As it was, when I kicked the thing, it travelled a quarter of the distance of anyone else's kick, and probably in the wrong direction. I didn't know what was wrong, and to this day, I have never discovered the answer. Much later, when serving with Indian troops, I did derive some pleasure from hockey, particularly six-a-side. This is played on a small pitch about the size of a tennis court, and one can cannon the ball off the low wall surrounding the pitch. It is much faster than ordinary hockey, and that is perhaps why I was better at it; there was no time to think or position oneself; the ball either came in one's direction or not, so that one's play was more or less cut and dried. On a full-size hockey pitch, as with soccer and rugby, I could never anticipate, thus I nearly always managed to put myself in the wrong position, and ended up trying to make a futile dive at the ball when off-balance, going the wrong way. My sport was not a success story. Discounting my pony club blue and red rosettes, won at the Cattistock and Seavington Hunt gymkhanas, my sole sporting trophy was one minuscule cup won for swimming – back stroke, of all things. I must have been the wrong shape!

And so the coin fell. Heads or tails? Tails, or was it heads? In the longer term, it was heads. My experiences were invaluable, and have served me in good stead in later years.

This then, is why you are reading about an Erk's progress, instead of the 'Memoirs of a Royal Signals Officer'.

'Come on lad. Get fell in, or you will be AWOL.' (Absent without leave).

Chapter 3

STAND BY YOUR BEDS

Following my eighteenth birthday, on a day in August 1940, I gathered myself up, collected a few possessions, got into the car and was driven to Bristol by my stepfather. He delivered me at the entrance to the recruiting office. I walked through the door. He drove away and that was that.

Erk was at the starting gate.

Erk was off . . . Erk led the field – from the rear.

Apart from Guildford I was ignorant of big cities and therefore somewhat rudderless. I cannot possibly remember, in detail, the ritual that ensued; I had to take my oath of allegiance, but that must have been later. Accommodation for the night was in a large hall, with many others. We were free to do what we liked for the rest of the day, so I went to the theatre; Godfrey Tearle and Angela Baddeley in *The Light that Failed*. I assume it was a dramatisation of Kipling's book, and I know that I thoroughly enjoyed it. I was batty about the cinema, and to be able to go to live theatre was a great bonus.

When a sufficient number of recruits had been lined up, we were formed into a party and despatched to RAF Cardington in Bedfordshire – home of the two large hangars which housed the ill-fated airships R100 and R101, and which was now the depot for barrage balloons.

The first days at Cardington involved kitting out and selection of men to their future roles in the RAF. I had no idea of what I wanted to do. My whole approach was negative. When I reached the selection desk, I mumbled something about being a pilot, but when told that I could not be selective, that it was air crew or nothing, I said pilot or nothing. There was no encouragement to pursue that line of thought, so I suppose the selection team assessed that they had a pretty useless bit of British youth in front of them. That avenue turned into a cul-de-sac.

'What trade do you want to be?'

'I don't know.'

'Well, you had better make your mind up, or you will be GD.'

'GD – what's that?'

'General Duties – batman, orderly, cleaning the latrines and anything no one else wants to do.'

'No thanks.'

'Instrument mechanic?'

'No.'

'Armourer?'

'No.'

'Engine fitter?'

'No. I don't know one end of an engine from another.'

And so it went on.

No dogs, no cats, no countryside. Oh dear! I was lost.

Eventually, the word 'wood' was mentioned in connection with aircraft rigger. I had done woodwork at school, so here was something familiar.

Yes, I would be a rigger, so my fate was sealed.

Cardington was the basic training depot. Three weeks initiation into the RAF – a sort of sausage machine, in at one end looking sloppy, and out at the other end in blue uniform having been introduced to those endearing orders: 'Attention,' 'Stand at ease,' 'Left turn, right turn, about turn,' and 'You dozy little man, don't you know your right from your left?'

A little bit of first aid, a bit of hygiene, a visit to the dentist, FFI (Free from Infection) inspection; and joy of joys, the immunisation session – smallpox vaccination, TAB, TT plus a lot of other injections at the same time. The treatment was so drastic that we were given 48 hours in which to crawl onto our beds and moan. Total rest from the vociferous Sergeant and Corporal for two whole days.

Saturday. The Big Day. Barrack room inspection and ceremonial parade.

'Stand by your beds.' We had spent the whole of Friday evening spitting and polishing the barrack room; linoleum buffed to a glittering shine, windows cleaned, ablutions scrubbed out. THE MORNING came, our lockers were open so that the inspecting officer could see that every shirt and item of clothing was folded to within the 5 degree tolerance. The beds lined up in serried ranks, with sheets and blankets folded to equally meticulous margins.

'Ahhhh! Who forgot to clean behind his bed then? I can see dust.'

If, heaven forbid, our standard was not good enough, then it meant a further inspection on Saturday evening or on Sunday, and this put paid to going out of camp.

The parade was equally exacting with its inspection of personal turnout and drill.

'Hair cut, hair cut, hair cut.'

'What happened to your boots, lad?'

Is it surprising that ex-service men of that vintage had a bearing about them not found in later generations?

All good fun in retrospect, but we wondered at the time how it was helping the war effort. I hit a high spot on the drill square at one moment; a runner was required when we were in the middle of rifle drill and RHB was singled out because he was smarter than the rest of the sleepy squad.

There wasn't much time to turn round during the three weeks at Cardington. We were kept busy, shades of Arthur Askey 'Busily doing nothing' – productive. But on Saturday afternoons we were allowed to go into Bedford. There must have been a theatre there because once again I made a bee-line for it. *Lilac Time*. A sloppy story built round Shubert's music, but I enjoyed it. I can't believe that I did not inhabit the cinema, too, whenever possible. What else was there for a non-drinking, non-womanising Erk to do? A lot of the lads had enjoyed both experiences so I just kept my mouth shut. I had a lot to learn.

It was not surprising that I found myself keeping company with an entirely different set of people from ones I was used to. At school, I had played an insignificant role, but I had mixed with boys from similar backgrounds to my own. That did not mean that we necessarily got on well with one another, but we spoke the same language and used the same vocabulary. Don't get me wrong, I am not decrying any section of society; I am merely making the point that if one is accustomed to one set of values, it can be somewhat traumatic to find oneself surrounded on all sides by strangeness. To quote just one example of what I mean. There was one particular recruit in the barrack room who came from Reading. He was a man of the world (i.e. Reading!) who was never at a loss for words – and most of them began with 'f'. He was drinker, womaniser and all else besides. I was a shadow beside him and longed to have his personality – but not what went with it. Thinking back, nearly every sentence uttered in that barrack room contained the 'f' word, probably two or three times.

I could 'become one of them'; to adopt the same language and behaviour. They were young men with far more to them than I: self-possession, confidence and know-how. I had no doubt in my mind that these were the men the British nation was made of. I felt inadequate beside them. I knew enough history to realise this, and wished that I was part of it. But to have deserted my own standards would have been wrong, and I had no intention of doing so.

As an aside I would comment that I disapprove most strongly of the amount of barrack-room language used on television these days. Do not imagine that I am shocked. I can give as good as I get any day. But I deeply resent the involuntary penetration into my own drawing room of, not only this deplorable language, but the grunts and groans as well. Agree with me or not, television does set an example, and every display of this conduct imperceptibly releases another notch of self-control. It is the path, not to the fragile plateau of civilisation, but back into the jungle. It is highly offensive to quite a large percentage of the population, and it is time for the PC Brigade to latch onto this one. My stepfather possessed as good a vocabulary of rude language – in Hindi as well as English – as you might find anywhere, and yet I never once heard him use it in his own drawing-room. The Services have a good mellowing process for etiquette. Progress from the ranks upwards is through the Corporals' Mess, the Sergeants' Mess to the Officers' Mess. The intermediaries act as a leavening process so that on reaching the latter, the correct behaviour is recognised. There is nothing whatsoever to be said against fluidity in the social structure. It has always happened – and a good thing too – but I am old-fashioned enough to ask that graduation up the ladder be accompanied by the standards that go with it. I have no wish to be returned to the barrack room through television (or the Booker prize).

I made good friends, though I suppose not all that close, with many of my barrack room companions. I was very pally with a rough diamond from the north. He smoked like a chimney, his fingers were stained yellow with nicotine and he stank of cigarettes. I don't know why we were friendly; I suppose we must have had some things in common, but friends we were.

By and large, I kept myself to myself. I often went into town alone at week-ends and, in fact, my whole behaviour was likened to a snail: I carried my home on my back and withdrew into it when things were not quite to my liking. This was one of the great advantages of having been at boarding school. I entered into the Services with experience of having survived in my own way. Without this experience I am sure I should have sunk. As it was I was quite capable of bobbing about like a cork in a rough sea, and keeping afloat.

September 1940. The war was celebrating its first birthday, but to this nineteen-year-old it was little more than words; words spoken over the wireless, or written in the newspaper. The newsreel at the cinema painted a picture, but it was no closer to me than the Sino-Japanese war. In Dorset, life had continued as before. Now things were going to change.

From 1939 onwards, it was a dark world when the sun went down. The black-out. The yell, 'Put that light out'.

Admittedly, having lived most of my life in the country, I was quite used to darkness. Bed time in winter was to the light of a solitary candle (which blew out if one was not careful when passing through a doorway). On more than one occasion I negotiated the half-mile walk from home to Coles Cross on a pitch-dark night with no moon or stars. Even before 1939, looking out of the window revealed only a thin sprinkling of lights over three miles of countryside. At home the black-out was not a terribly serious handicap; we had shutters on the downstairs windows, so there was no need to worry about black-out screens. Going to bed with one candle behind drawn curtains was not likely to act as path-finder to the Luftwaffe. Using the car was a bit of an adventure, but a combination of petrol rationing plus black-out considerably reduced the number of nocturnal journeys. Cars had to black out. A hood was fitted over the (free-standing, not built-in) headlamps which allowed just a narrow slip of light to illuminate the road. Progress was thus slow, but with nothing else on the road, the only real hazard was the ditch!

By September 1940, when I was at Cardington, England was virtually one big blackness at night. Then the air-raids started. The night sky over London, some thirty miles distant, was a red glow. We came out of our barrack huts and watched the distant inferno and, for the first time, most of us realised that a real war was actually on. For the lads whose homes were in London, it must have been a terrible experience.

On our final weekend at Cardington we were given a forty-eight hour pass. I decided to visit my two aunts in Guildford, which meant going into London and out again. I saw the indomitable population taking shelter in the Underground. People everywhere with bedding and provisions, entertaining themselves and adapting to their new emergency home. Having negotiated the tube journey, I boarded the train at Waterloo, only to have to get out at Vauxhall Bridge to travel by bus to Clapham Junction. The line had been bombed.

I was lucky. I had to endure such excursions only occasionally, unlike the people who lived for five years under them. When these people emerged into fresh air the following morning, would there still be a home to go to? Or would it be a heap of rubble?

At the end of three weeks, how did we look, this gang of recruits? We knew every square yard of the parade ground, having passed over every one of them at slow time, quick time, and double time. Even our hands were familiar with small patches where we had been encouraged to display our manhood doing press-ups. No longer did our bodies lean forward with hands in pockets. Our shoulders were back, our chests were out, our stomachs were in, our hair was cut, our boots shone, and our uniforms were pressed. Each one of us was the very model of a military man.

And so it was, that having completed this training we entrained for Tring.

Tring had not entered my education up to that time; it could have been at the north pole for all I knew, but I now discovered that it was in Buckinghamshire and served the RAF Apprentice School at Halton, a school which also trained riggers and fitters. This was to be the next target in the first metamorphosis of RHB.

Halton lay on the edge of the Chiltern Hills, close to Wendover, with Aylesbury as the rallying place for Saturday afternoon passes. I must confess that I enjoyed Halton. We were in good barracks, well served by canteens and clubs, with a good train service to London and all stations to my home in Dorset. This latter amenity was all important for forty-eight hour passes, issued every four weeks.

I liked the surrounding countryside too. Plenty of woods clothed the hills, and I explored on hired (they must have been) bicycles, on Sundays. I was fortunate in having some distant relatives living at Great Missenden which was within easy cycling distance. Nothing gave me greater pleasure than wandering round their fields. He, blessed with the name Bazzard married she – a Brazil, thus when Blizard joined the company for Sunday lunch, we were all at 'Bs' and 'Zs'!

I spent six months at Halton training as an aircraft rigger. I feel sure that some of my readers will know little more about aircraft than that they fly and cart tens of thousands of people all over the world. To passengers, the mechanics of their transport is unfamiliar. I will therefore spend a few moments explaining the need for riggers.

An aircraft is a flying box. It is filled with all sorts of technical equipment. Such equipment is built, maintained and serviced in workshops, quite independent of its host. Only in the very final stage is it bolted into place in the aircraft. Each equipment, whether it be radio, radar, armament, instrument or whatever, is a study of its own, and therefore requires specialised tradesmen in its own field. These were the trades which I rejected at the selection desk.

Responsibility for airworthiness of the actual flying box rested with two trades – the engine fitter and the rigger. As the name implies, the engine fitter's task was to make sure the engine worked – everything from stripping it down to its component parts, re-building, re-installation, tuning and sensitivity of controls.

Responsibility for all the rest of the basic aircraft fell to the rigger, and this embraced a very wide range of items, ranging from cable controls of working surfaces, hydraulics of the undercarriage and wing flaps, to the repair of any damage to the fuselage. In fact, the total serviceability of the 'box'.

I think no aeronautical engineer would dispute my contention that the decade from early thirties to early forties was a time of intense aircraft development. Up to that time, almost all aircraft were bi-planes, constructed of wood. I believe the Faery Battle was one of the earliest RAF monoplanes. Planes with wooden frames were covered with doped canvas, and in the case of bi-planes, the wings were critically tuned to one another by wires which had to be adjusted to the correct tension. The Supermarine Spitfire, which soared to its record breaking speed in the 1931 Schneider Trophy ushered in a new era.

In 1940, the armed services were flying aircraft of various vintages, which in turn meant that tradesmen working on them had to be skilled in all aspects of all these aircraft constructions. The rigger's course, which I attended, reflected this need.

I have no intention of now embarking my reader on a rigger's mini-course; however, I believe it will be of interest to many to learn the scope of accomplishment of the good old Erk, during his twelve week course.

I think I have made it plain that my own technical knowledge at that time was nil. My stepfather possessed not a morsel of mechanical ability. To insert a nail into a piece of wood was stretching him to the utmost. My mother was also a non-technical person, so that I had been set no example, or interest, to follow. At school, apart from woodwork – on which I was very keen – my technical world ended with a bit of bookbinding and printing. One might therefore say that I started at Halton with a clean slate.

I make no bones about it, I found the course absorbing. The instruction was excellent. The subjects were interesting and the personal achievement in turning out good 'apprentice pieces' was most rewarding. I enjoyed using my hands, and all the theoretical instruction was directly related to the practical work. I still carry many of the skills with me – in my head, if not in practice.

Aircraft maintenance cannot afford to be slipshod. Should something go wrong with a motor car, the engine will stop and one will coast gently to the side of the road. A call to the AA or a little self-help will solve the problem. One can continue on one's way at the price of only lost time and dirty hands. The same fault in an aircraft will result in a crash with drastic consequences. As a generalisation, one can say that any man (or woman) who has worked on aircraft is a thorough tradesman given to complete reliability. If, in the day-to-day problem of looking after your house, you can find an all-round workman who has worked on aircraft, then my advice is to hang onto him like grim death. He is worth his weight in gold.

Because our aircraft of that time were of so many types of construction, the rigger had to know them all. The Spitfire had a metal fuselage, while the Hurricane was of wood and canvas. The Wellington and Westland Lysander were of geodetic construction (a 12" crisscross of light metal – duralumin – spars covered with canvas.) Great chunks of these two aircraft could be shot away, but they would still fly. We had to be able to carry out repairs to metal, wood and canvas – and the joints had to be perfect. A set-square was an important tool. I was given the task of shaping a block of mild steel into a neat oblong with square sides, then the instructor ran his set-square over every edge to check my accuracy.

At the outset we were taught the theory of flight; how lift was achieved from the aerodynamic cross-section of the wings; why the Lysander had a lower stalling speed than that of the Spitfire. In fact, we were taught all the essential background knowledge so that we fully understood the importance of every aspect of our rigger work.

Aircraft controls were stranded steel cable. We had to be able to make them ourselves. This required splicing. We worked on rope, then graduated to steel; using a marlin-spike we terminated cables around eyelets, and jointed them. It was fascinating, and many years later I believe this is one of the reasons why I enjoy making anti-pigeon nets for my garden.

Hydraulics. Science at school had taught me a bit about blocks and pulleys, but I had not discovered the power of hydraulics. Seal some oil in a circuit, insert a few valves, and you can move a mountain with no effort, but total accuracy. There were demonstration bench layouts of the systems used in the aircraft. We had to replace sections of 'damaged' piping, tap and die new connections, then stand back and have our work checked.

Aircraft undercarriages. Oleo legs. The force with which an aircraft hits the ground on the runway is not generally realised. It is a small miracle that two, four, or more spindly little legs can withstand such an impact. They take the shock, are concertina-ed, but then return to their expanded position to sustain further buffeting. All done through hydraulics in a long cylinder. We learned about them, and how to detect faults.

As I have said, I lapped up this knowledge and these skills. I passed out at the end of the course with a sufficiently good mark to ensure a place in the follow-on course for the next grade. Regrettably, my achievement on this latter course was not up to the same standard. I have no reason for believing that I malingered, so I suppose I had reached saturation point. I needed live practical work before absorbing more teaching under laboratory conditions.

Away from the training school, life for an Erk was much the same as life for any other ranker. I cannot remember how miscellaneous duties were arranged to fit in with the training schedule, but we had our fair share of fatigues and guard duties. I came to know the cookhouse quite well! There always seemed to be an awful lot of cleaning up to be done, vast pans which required scalding out, and acres of stone floor to be swilled down. The chores came round all too frequently, but there were some perks too – fried bread and eggs between meals!

Guards and picket duties were always on the menu. That delightful two-hour period between two and four a.m. when everyone else was asleep, and one longed to join them. Even standing up induced somnolescence. By counting the windows of the barracks and such-like mental activities, one tried to keep alert, but occasionally one's head would nod.

When one's name appeared on DROs (Daily Routine Orders) for guard duties, there was a glimmer of hope. One extra man was always nominated, so that when the initial guard was mounted and inspected by the duty officer, one fortunate man would be selected for the leisurely duty of 'stick-man'. He was the smartest on parade and was either dismissed altogether, or allocated a waiting role so that he could snore peacefully while the less fortunate stood awake.

Chance played a part in this lottery. A quick study of the names on DROs gave one a good indication of one's hopes. Some Erks were professional 'stick-men'; their boots possessed a higher gleam, their trouser creases were more acute, brasses had an extra glitter, and the heel came down with a louder crash when we had the order 'about turn'. Against such odds one had no hope. I am glad to report that just occasionally I was the lucky man – not often, but enough to keep my end up.

I cannot leave Halton without some reference to off-duty activities. There was a cinema in camp which changed the programme two or three times a week, so that took care of an equal number of evenings. The NAAFI was a thriving concern. Even though the RAF supplied us with a hefty evening meal, the tum was rattling again by 8.30, so there was an everlasting demand for eggs, bacon and sausage, swilled down with a mug of sweet tea. I was a non-drinker, but anyway, I am pretty sure no beer was dispensed in barracks. There were other canteens within the overall camp boundary so that we could ring the changes.

Particular highlights were the entertainments offered to the troops by ENSA and like bodies. We had a good ration of them. I will always remember my first live concert, given by the RAF orchestra; it did all the things to me that people say music can do. I also discovered the Amersham Repertory Company and managed to attend one or two Saturday matinee performances, *Blythe Spirit* among them.

Apart from that, my main occupation was reading. I quickly acquired the ability to sit/lie on my bed reading, to the total oblivion of all other goings-on in the barrack room. Lights out was at 10.30, so I usually had at least an hour's reading time, even if I had been to the cinema.

Saturday afternoon usually took the form of a bus ride to Aylesbury. My first stop was the book shop where I stocked up for the next week. This was followed by canteen and/or cinema, perhaps in the company of another lad from the camp. It wasn't a bad life. We would not have been normal if we had not ticked like meters. We found plenty to grumble about, but I am sure that I am not the only ex-Erk to look back at Halton with some nostalgia.

It came to an end. 17 April 1941. At the end of the course I was nominated for overseas, with a temporary posting to St Eval in Cornwall.

Chapter 4

ALL ABOARD

ENSA Concert

So far, so good, let the saga begin – a saga written in misspelt manuscript by the same hand that, now fifty-five years on, transposes it into this book. The same hand. The same person? Yes and no. Much that was evident all those years ago is still present, but it was a different life. Were it not for three exercise books recording the day by day events for a period of twelve months, most of it would have been lost. Never happened? But it did happen – I have evidence of it. Furthermore, by handling these words written so long ago, memory is jogged and I can recall other events as bear witness to the amount I am able to fill in from my diary.

St Eval, Cornwall. 14th May 1941.
After three whole days' leave, I return to St Eval for overseas posting. Saying goodbye wasn't much fun, but by the time I reached Exeter I had recovered. My chief reaction after this leave is that I should go

abroad as soon as possible, without further delay – anyway, without going home again.

Upon reaching the camp, I found that my hut was destroyed and everyone billeted out. I was really rather pleased that my hut was bombed while I was away. I waited in the guard room for transport to Porth; a WAAF was there who was drunk.

A party of us had been posted from Halton to St Eval to await our drafting overseas, thus St Eval was little more than a transit camp. Following official embarkation leave of about 10 days, our time alternated between further batches of two or three days leave, and some occasional work on aircraft.

When we arrived the airfield was running smoothly, but then it, along with other places in the south west, became a target for German bombing. On arrival we all lived in camp, but as a result of the bombing all except essential staff were found billets in Newquay and the surrounding area. During my absence, my own hut was bombed and it was with some glee that I stood where my bed had been and looked at the tangled wreckage which remained.

15 May 1941.
I reported to the orderly room at 9 o'clock and was told I could have the day off, but must be prepared to go next day. I secured a bed for the night, then went into Newquay. A man stopped me and asked me to look at his garden. He wished me the best of luck, as did one or two other people.

As far as I can remember, the billeting was a bit of a free-for-all. We were driven from camp in a lorry and dropped off at random. From my diary I assume that my first night was spent in the first bed that was found, but after that I remained in the same house. To be wearing uniform ensured a welcome everywhere. Total strangers in town, village or country would stop to talk, and it was not unusual to be invited in for a cup of tea.

16 May 1941.
I reported to the orderly room this morning but was told to go away and come back tomorrow. They might have extended our leave instead of leaving us waiting here.

All the same, I was delighted to have this time to myself. I had never been to Cornwall before this posting. I found this north coast gorgeous. Porth island was joined to the mainland by a little bridge, and I loved it, with the seagulls above and the sea beating against the cliffs at one's feet. By this time I had explored the coast a bit. Our original arrival for St Eval had been by train to Padstow – a fascinating train journey followed by first sight of this delightful little fishing port.

During my spare time I had walked and discovered this magnificent coastline. Bedruthan Steps hits the headlines, but there is not much wrong with the rest. I made a resolve that I would return to the area after the war. Something I did in 1948 when, together with an RAF officer, we took our bicycles to Padstow by train, then cycled down the north coast to Lands End, and back along the south coast of Cornwall, Devon and Dorset to my home in Dorset. I do not have space here to tell that story, enough to say that St Eval whetted my appetite for 'adventure'.

17 May 1941.
I reported to the orderly room this morning but was told to go away. In order to get out of the camp without being detailed for clearing up debris from last night's air-raid, four of us made a detour via the perimeter track.

Clearing up the debris after the raid required a fatigue party. Life in the Services without fatigue parties would have been like a car without an engine. During my two years in the RAF I spent many hours doing fatigues, swilling out cookhouses, peeling potatoes, polishing linoleum, clearing up rubbish – you name it. It was part of life and whilst being a chore at the time, helped to make us clean, tidy and self-respecting. We could do with a little more of this nowadays.

18 May 1941.
As usual I made my report to the orderly room this morning. In the evening I was hungry so walked into Newquay and had chicken for supper.

This reference to chicken has stirred the memory. Somewhere, so it must have been St Eval because I did not serve on any other UK airfield, I worked on Wellington and Hampden bombers. They were dispersed round the edge of the field; the weather was windy and wet. There was a farmhouse near the perimeter and we riggers and fitters used to evacuate to the farm kitchen where the farmer's wife fed us on poached eggs on toast for a very modest sum. This brightened up both mornings and afternoons. I feel sure the good lady must be deceased by now, but just in case she is not, and happens to read this book, then I thank her for the comfort she gave us.

Eating was essential to a young serviceman. Small cafés or canteens were an important part of life. Canteens were in operation all over the country wherever soldiers, sailors, or airmen were to be found. Many organisations ran these canteens – Salvation Army, Red Shield, YMCA, plus many more including quite a lot of voluntary ones. They formed a hub for service life, and to their unsung staff, every serviceman was eternally grateful.

37

In my first days at St Eval I had walked much of the coastal path and on one occasion I was in need of refreshment. I espied a smart looking hotel so made my way towards it. I was barred entry. The establishment was out of bounds to other ranks, only officers could enter its portals. I was put out, but had to accept the situation. All the same, I could not help wondering what would have happened had I been in the company of my stepfather – Colonel retired, with airman. With maturity one can see the point of such rules. In the context of 1940, when politeness and courtesy were the order of the day, to have mixed officers with loud mouthed f...ing other ranks would have been disastrous, but not all other ranks were of that ilk. As with all rules, the blanket treatment is unfair – but then, life as a whole is unfair, and always will be.

19 May 1941.
Another holiday. I went to Truro. I was lifted both ways, four times going, six returning (3 lorries, 3 cars).

For journeys long or short, uniform was a passport for a lift. Many drivers would always offer lifts. For example, Newcastle could be reached from any point on the Great North Road almost as quickly as by train. For many of the lads, hitchhiking was the normal mode of transport.

20th May 1941.
As usual I phoned the orderly room with the same result. I stopped to talk to the woman who owns the house. Really, the government's behaviour is disgusting. What it amounts to is that she was turned out [of her own house] by fraudulent methods and, of course, she can't do anything about it.

I cannot remember why I became so indignant on behalf of my landlady.

I think the area was thrown into turmoil as a result of the bombing and something had to be done quickly to accommodate a horde of servicemen. No doubt the people who arranged this billeting were heavy handed, but what could one expect under the circumstances?

21 May 1941.
I rang the orderly room, but contrary to the usual run of things I was told that our postings had come through, and that we were to report with full kit to Station as soon as possible. When we reached the orderly room at midday we were told to come back at 2.30, when we were given our paybooks. In the meantime I tried to acquire the deficiencies on my kit list, without any luck. At last we started, leaving the camp at 3.30 to catch the 4.45 from Newquay. A Sergeant was in charge of our party but of all the nit-wits, he was the biggest – when we reached Bristol he made us change into a train which went to Manchester, then into another for Birmingham, changing there, then changing again at Crewe.

We passed through Plymouth on the way and I must admit that Jerry had made a nasty mess of it.

A paybook was an all important document; without it one virtually lost one's identity. It recorded one's rate of pay, next of kin, personal number and other essential information. One never departed one's unit without it. While on the strength of a unit the document spent part of its life in the orderly room and pay office, otherwise in one's own possession.

Travelling was a circuitous operation. One rarely travelled by the quickest route; no doubt, this was to avoid congestion on the main arteries, but to us Erks, it seemed a very round-about way of doing things. And of course, on these mass movements one's destination as often as not, remained a mystery. It was a bit hard to blame the Sergeant who was only carrying out his orders!

22 May 1941.
The advent of Thursday saw me endeavouring unsuccessfully to sleep on the train. A difficult procedure. At last we got to Wilmslow at 10 o'clock, and marched up to the camp. We were given a bed, then went for a meal – the best RAF one since I left Halton. After this meal I went to sleep for a couple of hours, then I enjoyed a beautiful hot bath. All our entry [riggers] seem to be turning up here by degrees.

Newquay to Crewe, say 300 miles. It took us 17 hours. Not bad going!
Life was one long uncertainty. Apart from the fact that we knew we were going overseas, we had no idea when or where we were going. At this stage we could have been bound for the North Pole or anywhere else you like to mention.

23 May 1941.
The first full day at Wilmslow. The food is definitely very good, and the whole camp is pretty efficient, though compared with a Squadron there is a great deal of red tape. This morning we were issued with tropical kit, which for a moment, made me homesick. After lunch we were given a lecture on secrecy and other subjects. I went to a concert this evening.

The issue of tropical kit indicated a general direction of movement – Middle East or Far East? The concert was variety and included Tessy O'Shea: a large lady who swung on a swing. This provided us with additional entertainment in the back row; we wondered if the CO in the

40

front row might receive her in his lap.

24 May 1941.

Today I have been on 'Stretcher Bearer Squad' for 24 hours – particularly unlucky on a Saturday because we miss our half-day off, but Manchester has been out of bounds so it doesn't matter all that much.

It has been announced on the wireless this evening that H.M.S. Hood has been sunk. I certainly don't think this war will be over by the end of the year, as some people say.

25 May 1941.

We have not had any serious duty and I have been out all the afternoon and evening. This morning, we had to hand in our second pair of boots, but otherwise there were no parades.

26 May 1941.

A marching day. This morning we had about 1 hour's marching on the square, then this afternoon we went for a route march in the surrounding countryside.

I sent off my case at last.

The case contained surplus gear not being taken overseas. I sent it home by rail.

27 May 1941.

The Air Force is inefficient. I should not have believed it possible for anything to be run so badly. This morning at 10.30 I started my 'respirator chase'. By 12.15 a small amount had been achieved, namely a great many visits to a great many people all of whom were incapable of doing anything. This afternoon we propped up the stores for 2 hours with no result; the outcome of all this is that the same performance starts again tomorrow.

For the rest of the day, the first hour was rifle drill – which proved more amusing than anything else.

From the nineteen nineties, it is difficult to believe that time was ever such an unimportant commodity. A whole lot of men had to be kept out of mischief for 24 hours a day, so the problem was what to do with them. Going round the camp on a 'respirator chase' was as good as anything else. In the hands of inexperienced junior NCOs, some of our parade ground activities were a lark.

28 May 1941.
More chasing respirators with equally inspiring results. This morning we were issued with berth tickets so that we should be prepared to go at any moment – rumour has it, Friday.

We only had to march once round the camp during the whole day. This afternoon the NCOs were tired so we spent the afternoon as we liked.

Another tedious day.

29 May 1941.
At long last the respirator has materialised after the corporal blasted the stores.

It seems fairly well assured that we leave here tomorrow; it will be exactly six weeks after leaving Halton, and an excellent six weeks from my point of view. I have had no proper work to do but I have been paid 4/9 per day irrespective of everything; this is a wonderful idea as far as I am concerned but I do not see how we shall win the war if similar things continue. Yet another concert tonight, the best so far.

My time in Newquay had given me the first real freedom of my life – and I received pay for it. My childhood and youth had been closely supervised at home, and no school is freedom. Cardington and Halton were organised almost to the minute, so that for the first time in my life, after reporting to the orderly room in the morning, I had total uncluttered freedom for the rest of the day. I revelled in it.

Most concerts took the form of variety turns. This particular one included two singers who sang the 'Miserere' from *Il Trovatore*. I thought it wonderful, and I am sure it contributed to my on-going love of opera.

Everyone knows all about ENSA. It did a wonderful job. Groups reached the smallest military units in the remotest places, and they boosted morale no end. Big names too – Noel Coward to 14th Army; his singing of 'London Pride' is something all of us can never forget. These entertainers made an enormous contribution to the troops well-being, in every theatre of war. In India, I can remember laughing my head off at some really futile jokes; but that did not matter; the 'feel-good' factor – to use a modern phrase – should never be de-bunked. Another time, a touring company staged Shaw's *Arms and the Man*. It went down very well.

30 May 1941
Contrary to all expectations we have not started on our 'world cruise' today. Instead we are told that it will be early Monday morning. This morning we started off with rifle drill, followed by PT, followed by nothing at all except reading.

One was living from day-to-day in a sort of limbo. No certainty or particular aim in life.

1st June 1941.

This is supposedly our last day in England and perhaps why we have been confined to camp. For some obscure reason we had to move our lodgings today, only a matter of 50 yards but it took a complete hour at least. Have written to Eleanor [an aunt] asking for the *Works of Masefield.*

We were all facing the unknown. We had none of us ever been to sea before. We didn't know where we were going or what to expect when we arrived. We were killing time.

Eleanor duly sent the book to me, overseas. Fifty years on and I have it still.

I have recently re-read *The Widow of Bye Street* – a sorry tale; and *Reynard the Fox.* This latter is a wonderful word picture, but I have always looked upon it as a bit of a cheat. For seventy-two pages, one is taken through the whole hunt: 'But still, needs must when the devil drives'. Then . . . on the 73rd page:

> 'But the cry of the hounds was not for him.
> Over the fence with a crash they went,
> Belly to grass with a burning scent . . .'

The hounds take on a new scent and our fox escapes. Masefield avoids the kill. I would probably have done the same, but he did not evade the hanging in the 'Widow', so why not the killing of a fox in 'Reynard'?

2 June 1941.

Whitsun, and we have the pleasure of arriving at ?, our port of embarkation. After a remarkably restless night caused by Jerry and his raids, we left Wilmslow at 8.30 dressed up like mules. The weight of those packs is pretty terrific – at least, after it has been on one's back for some time. For once the RAF has excelled itself and sent us to the nearest port instead of the other end of the island.

The boat – or should I say ship – isn't too big and we are squashed in like sardines, but on the whole it isn't as bad as it might be. It surprises me how small all the ships are; a destroyer passed us and it is astonishingly small. I now begin to appreciate the defeat of the *Graf Spree*.

If we were now told that we were not going overseas, I would be most disappointed. I have been living in expectation for the last six weeks so that an anticlimax would really be an anticlimax. We did not have any duties during the day except 'scuttle procedure'. This ship is on its first troop voyage so that we have found a certain amount of chaos, especially with regard to food. For the night we moved away from the quay into the river – no doubt to avoid bombs.

The port was Liverpool. A serviceman on the move had to carry all his own kit. It was distributed about his person – in a small haversack hanging at his side, containing immediate necessities (balanced by a full water-bottle on the other side), his backpack containing less immediate necessities, and his kitbag containing more long-term essentials and luxuries. A book worm was at a disadvantage; paper weighs, but I was not going to travel without the nucleus of a library.

And so, 'Goodbye England'. I would not see you again for another four years, and during that time anything could happen.

In fact I returned as a Captain . . . in the Army!

Chapter 5

AT SEA – TO CAPE TOWN

SS *Eastern Prince*, of the Prince Line (Furnace Withy & Co). Her house insignia was the Prince of Wales Feathers, which she proudly bore, emblazoned on her funnel. She was to be our mobile home for the next nine weeks.

She was launched in 1929, and until this first trooping voyage, she had plied the South America run as a cargo passenger vessel, carrying Argentine beef. At 11,000 tons she had six holds which had been converted into troop accommodation. Each hold housed about 150 men, so including the crew and independent RAF officers in transit, her total compliment was about 1,500 souls.

The holds were very cramped. Mess tables seating twenty men each, ten per side, projected inwards from the shell of the ship. Each table had a bench fixed on either side for seating. There must have been about ten tables per hold. There was locker space in each hold for stowing our immediate necessity kit. Our kit bags were elsewhere. At night we swung our hammocks on the hooks of the upper bulkhead in line fore and aft. A hammock occupied twice its sleeping length, so each line of hammocks was suspended from alternate lines of hooks; thus one row of hammock 'heads' lined up with the next row of hammock 'tails' to form a solid sea of hammocks across the entire hold area.

As one descended the companionway down into the hold, the effect was of a gentle swell of canvas moving in sympathy with the ship. The sleeping contents would raise the occasional arm or foot above surface to remind one that human life was there. In truth, of course, the hammocks retained their vertical hanging position; it was the ship that moved around them.

3 June 1941.

The first night aboard was much less eventful than I expected. After the first few difficulties, the erection of the hammocks went quite smoothly. To start with, it was frightfully hot, but by the early morning it was much cooler.

Today broke dull and misty over the port and it did not brighten up until afternoon. We sailed at about 2.30 but we were not allowed on deck so that I missed seeing the last of England, except for a very faint line on the horizon. I am glad to be going. I haven't thought about home very much so that I have not been homesick. I have a feeling that I shall not be seasick either – in fact, up to date, I like the gentle heave. Tonight I queued up for three hours to get some chocolate – I shan't do it again unless I am desperate.

One of our first introductions to life on board was boat drill. We were allotted to an individual life-boat according to mess deck. This became our muster station where we would assemble in an emergency. In time of crisis, of course, such orderliness might not apply, but to have an automatic drill was obviously essential. The other potential life saver was to carry our Mae West life jackets with us at all times. This was a nuisance, but the bonus was that they made extremely good cushions when sitting on a hard deck for most of the day.

Having been detailed to our life-boat stations, this provided us with a sort of *pied-de-terre* on the ship, so that we mustered (or paraded) in front of our respective boat every morning. The roll was called (someone might have disappeared overnight!) and any orders for the day were announced.

4 June 1941.

We have been sailing west all day, but I do not feel as though we have really started yet. It all seems so fantastic and impossible to be leaving the country I have known all my life; I can't realise it.

Coming out on deck this morning Scotland was to starboard and Ireland to port. Later – about 9.30 we picked up another 12 ships outside Glasgow. Our convoy is pretty large. I have spent most of the day leaning on the rail watching the sea – it is fascinating. The water looks like mercury; it gives the impression of being so solid, or else it looks like silk being rubbed underneath by a stick. It can take any form in which the mind sees it.

Not being allowed on deck, we did not see how many ships left Liverpool with us, but by the time the Glasgow contingent joined us we must have been at least twenty. With hindsight, I wish I had recorded details of the convoy, but I didn't, so I must make do with memory – which is hazy.

We were a motley lot of vessels, of all sizes. The largest was the *Empress of Japan*. She was one of the nearest ships to us, and kept her place to our starboard. Each ship retained its position in the convoy, and we moved rather like a flock of starlings; if the leading vessel veered to the left, we all went that way, weaving our way across the ocean. Memory tells me that our naval escort consisted of a cruiser and three destroyers, but I may be wrong. The cruiser was HMS *Birmingham* (I think). The destroyers rushed about all over the place and one never knew where they were; *Birmingham* maintained a more dignified role and did less rushing.

Our speed was obviously geared to the slowest vessel, and I think it was about fifteen knots. I do not know naval tactics, but we probably kept wireless silence for most of the time, to avoid detection. We could see lamp signalling between vessels.

5 June 1941.
I can't make out where we are going. Tonight we are still travelling west. Iceland must be the nearest land by now. The sea is becoming rougher; in fact, this evening there has been one casualty (i.e. seasickness). Each day is very much the same: all I do is read, and lean on the rail.

I do not need to explain that this was the time of the Battle of the Atlantic, so no sea journey was straightforward. Not only were we in convoy, but our route was circuitous. Our first port of call was to be Freetown, about one week normal sailing time; but it took us two weeks. We went out well into the Atlantic before heading south, then approached Freetown from south of west. The next stage from Freetown to Capetown followed a similar pattern. Overall, we were actually at sea for 25 days from Liverpool to Capetown, plus three days at Freetown.

6 June 1941.
Our direction is now south. So far there is no sign of extra warmth. Towards evening, quite a swell has developed so that there is now

49

continual movement. I have not been seasick yet, but a fair number have been.

After tea I went along to the bow. There, the rise and fall is over ten feet. It is lovely standing there being lifted right up, then dropped down into the trough. It is possible to see barriers of water coming towards the ship so that one knows when to expect them – gorgeous.

I find it surprising that we were allowed onto the foredeck; but by the time the promenade deck was reserved for officers, there was not all that much space left for 900 other ranks. I suppose it was a forced decision to allow us there. I loved it. I found it exhilarating to lean over the rail and see the bow cutting through the water. On a flat sea, it was like a knife, smoothly cutting through butter, but the greater the swell, the greater the excitement. One could see the crest of the wave coming from afar, and know that as the ship met it, so the bow would rise into the air, then drop into the following trough. Looking over the side, one had a competition with oneself to identify the greatest rise and fall measured against the horizon.

7 June 1941.
These days at sea are all the same as one another – one continues to see the sea, the sky and the same faces, but little else. The storm has increased during the day so that there is now a distinct roll. This evening we have been told that we may write home. I have been told that I will do guard tomorrow. This is my first to date, which is very lucky.

By now we must be in the middle of the Atlantic and heading south because we are two hours behind English time. This is being righted one hour tonight.

Guard duties. They seemed to come round every four or five days, which was very frequent with 900 men aboard. However, quite a number of men were on permanent duties such as manning the orderly room, so I am sure it was all very fair. Anyway, Erks like me did guard duty – two hours on and four hours off for twenty-four hours at a time. There were guard posts in each of the holds plus quite a lot of other locations.

Why guards anyway? To keep us occupied. We were not a mischievous lot, but idleness bred trouble. We, all of us, from different stations in life, had a respect for discipline. Unlike modern youth we had all been brought up to do as we were told. Fathers featured at home, and they were not afraid to chastise wrong-doers. Not withstanding this, it was better to have as many men as possible 'doing' something rather than sitting idly about the deck. A mischief was less likely to happen on duty than off duty. Even though we were afloat normal military hierarchy prevailed. Wrong-doers were placed on a charge, marched in front of an officer and given jankers as appropriate. Irons were no longer in use to the best of my knowledge!

8 June 1941.
This has been the roughest day so far, but we hope that by the morning the storm will have blown itself out. I haven't enjoyed it so much today but it might have been much worse. I have been on solitary guard so perhaps that emphasised it – left alone to think of seasickness.

By now I should think we are as far south as Portugal or Gibraltar. It still doesn't seem as though we are miles away from England; it ought to be just over the horizon.

To the landlubber, apart from bangs in the night 'Home' is a silent place, (subject to noises actuated by man-handled switches!). But to the seafarer, life is different; noise is an indication that all is well. A ship has a heart which beats, whether this heart be sail, coal, steam, or even atoms. The pistons pound, giving the motive power, and the screws turn. One may not be conscious of these sounds, but as soon as they stop, the silence shouts.

There are other noises too, lost in the hubbub of daytime life, but coming into their own in the silent hours. On picket duty from two to four a.m. is the time to hear the full orchestra. The ship rolls from side to side, each roll accompanied by a prolonged creak, starting at one end of the roll, rising to a crescendo, then diminishing to almost zero; as the ship starts its reverse roll, so the creak replays in the opposite direction. All parts of the ship make their imperceptible contribution to the overall sound, and the rougher the sea, the louder the orchestration.

The creaking of a ship to a sailor must be as reassuring as the lowing of cattle is to a farmer.

A visible manifestation of this can be witnessed too. Picket duty is at one end of a long gangway. Looking for'ard (or aft as the case may be) the gangway spirals up and down, side to side. Hang a plumbline from the upper bulkhead, and the pattern would compare favourably with that drawn by a spirograph.

9 June 1941.

As we hoped, the storm has abated leaving us in a gorgeous blue sea with an equally blue sky. By midday we were beginning to find that the sun is somewhat hotter than it is back home. I lay in the sun for about one hour and to my surprise found my arms quite burnt.

During the night, while on guard I was almost ill but I managed to ride it off. Getting up at an unearthly hour without anything to eat did not help.

Tonight, we are told that tropical kit will be worn tomorrow so that everything below decks is chaos and scorching hot. The padre of the ship arranged a concert which relieved the monotony in the evening.

The first real sunshine. I was (am) a sun worshipper, and as a septuagenarian, it has so far, done me no harm in spite of what the experts say. My recipe is the more the better. I have spent many hours under a tropical sun dressed only in shorts, often less, sometimes nothing. My skin is so pigmented that it carries me forward from one year to the next.

There are some precautions to take. Cover the head, and slowly slowly does it. My one hour on deck was quite long enough for the first day, the same again next then I increased the dosage a little at a time. By the time I reached Port Suez, I was pretty well 'browned off'. It was worth it. There are few things to equal a tropical beach, in the hot sun, in and out of the water in the 'altogether', but it is essential to be brown by then or the lobster state ensues.

Altitude is another matter. Black though I was from tropical sun at sea level, Kashmir at 6,000 feet played havoc. A day lolling about on the Dal Lake, in a *shikara* (a boat), in the sun and I paid the price. My legs swelled up and the skin cracked open. It was very painful, and I had a huge blister across both my shoulders. I learned my lesson.

10 June 1941.
Last night was so hot that instead of sleeping down in the hold, I came up on deck and spent the night there. It was lovely sleeping under the starry sky and not at all uncomfortable. If only it weren't for the crowd, it would be perfect.

It was hot in the hold, even at UK latitude. As we went south, it became unbearable. Trying to sleep in a hammock, head to tail with the next bloke, was impossible. Thank goodness we were allowed on deck. Space was a problem but with luck, one managed to stake a claim; mine was on the boat deck, to windward of the funnel to avoid the fumes, unless there was too much wind in which case fumes won the night. The hardness of the deck was no problem. I had once spent a night at Yeovil Junction station sleeping on a 9" bench, so 15" was a luxury.

11 June 1941.
Absolutely nothing has happened today except that France has declared war on us. It makes one wonder if we shall reach our destination without encountering a French ship. We are told that we shall be calling at a port for fresh supplies within two or three days; however, we shall not be allowed ashore so it makes little difference.

Nowadays, one never considers darkness as a problem, there is not much of it. But it was important during the war, and as a convoy, we sailed in total darkness. Sandbag baffles hid light from doorways opening onto the deck. (Oh the joy in 1945 when I returned to the Far East after leave, on the SS *Johann Van Oldenbaneveldt*. The sandbags were dismantled on the voyage). Being mid-summer when we left England, the days were long and we were not inconvenienced at our own northern latitude, but the further south we went, the more heat increased and the nights lengthened. After dark the choice was a hot illuminated hold or a dark deck. The latter usually won.

12 June 1941.
My birthday, and I was on guard duty, so I spent various hours of the day propping up No. 6 hold wall. There is a fairly strong wind from the east; I shan't be at all surprised if we have another storm. For the rest, it is exactly the same as any other day, and I don't feel

much older either.

What can one say about a birthday even at the best of times? I will move on to the next day.

13 June 1941.
At an early hour a member of the crew pointed out that it was Friday the thirteenth, and so best to watch out. Nothing happened so the day has fallen a bit flat! The unusual occurrence has been that I have seen my first flying fish – they look very much like swallows except that they suddenly disappear into the water.

Today, I have had my first lesson at bridge – one game. In the evening I wrote a letter home, but it is too late to catch the post from this port.

Shipboard to me, means cards. Later, when commissioned, on the *Oldenbarneveldt*, we played bridge at all hours, but now, my experience was limited to rummy. I had graduated to solo, which involved a bit of bidding, so bridge was the next step, and never to be regretted. The fact that my friends, at the age of nineteen, were bridge players gives some indication of the company I was keeping.

14 June 1941.
No sign of land, although everybody says we are very close. We have been swerving about in all directions during the day owing to submarines from Dakar. Some people say they have seen sharks. I don't believe them. Bridge this evening. I understand the idea at last.

I have already told of my liking for the bow. The stern was equally

55

fascinating. One stood immediately above the propellers and watched the turbulence below, with the wake stretching backwards to the horizon in a straight line. But when we altered course the pattern changed. Mentally, one lifted oneself into the sky to see the wakes of all the vessels in the convoy forming circles on the ocean.

15 June 1941.
As hot as ever; playing cards and reading. It is thundery heat so one just perspires without doing anything.

16 June 1941.
Last night there was a thunderstorm. At 1.30 the storm broke, so that we were wet before we knew where we were. I spent the rest of the night in the hold and did not like it. Today, not much sun, but thoroughly sultry.

About 12 we sighted land. We approached the shore from the west, and watched the hills gradually growing larger. Soon I could detect an odd house or two buried in the vivid green hillsides. A pleasure steamer went past us on our starboard and various other craft were dotted about at intervals. The harbour itself is really an enormous bay, but apparently there is only a single channel into it. The pilot came aboard and we made our way in very slowly.

Just off the lighthouse point we could see the mast of a ship which had been sunk. The further we came inland the more we could see and it was very tempting. To the south, hills mount almost out of the sea, while the north-east is all lowland. The hills are covered by vivid green vegetation all up the slopes. Along the shore there are palms which come almost down to the shore. In one place there is a small lagoon which looks most tempting. Freetown seems quite small. It appears to consist of rows of houses with no chimneys and only slightly sloping roofs.

We anchored about 4.30, fairly far up-river amidst the rest of the convoy. A few native craft were sailing about but we did not see any very close. Night fell at 7 o'clock, but I remained on deck and watched the lights – the first I have seen since September 1939 – nearly two years ago. But for some reason or another, the blackout was enforced on our ship.

My first sight of tropical land. The cinema come to life and Somerset Maugham realised.

17 June 1941.

Again last night, there was a very heavy thunderstorm which drove us into the hold at about midnight. It has been my day for guard, but I haven't missed very much. When I emerged on deck, crowds were at the rail watching the natives, and buying fruit. They seem a peculiar race. They hang about and barter with their goods. They came in their narrow canoes which, I suppose, they build themselves, and they paddled back and forth shouting their wares. Laurie bought a couple of pineapples which we devoured later. The fruit is not quite as strong as the tinned variety, but that may be because it is unripe. The tide in the bay makes us swing round at anchor so that we face in all directions from time to time. In the afternoon the tanker came alongside and loaded us up; this took the whole afternoon.

For my guard I was in number 3 hold and I don't think I have ever been so hot before. I just stood and streamed. During the afternoon we played bridge.

18 June 1941.

My guard duty had got me thinking during the night. I walked along the deck and saw the officers asleep outside on deck, with sheets and camp beds and plenty of room. It seems wrong to me that 900 men should live in about 1/3rd of this ship, in its hottest parts, while 300 officers occupy 1/3rd. I do not mean that the difference between officers and men should not be considered, but at the same time I think a few comforts could be provided for us. e.g. more room and facilities for sitting down on deck. This afternoon we have had the most gorgeous storm in which I washed both myself and my clothes.

19 June 1941.
I have been exceptionally bored and unable to settle to anything.

20 June 1941.
When I came out on deck after lunch, I found that we were moving out of Freetown. We started to sail at 1 o'clock. As we passed the town it seemed to be much larger than it had previously appeared. It was possible to see a train and a few vehicles passing through the trees by the shore. The convoy is about the same size as the last; there are just a few alterations in the ships. I am not sure if I am pleased or sorry to be leaving here, it means that it will be a more bearable temperature but at the same time it means that we shall reach our destination sooner. I felt a bit homesick last night, but I suppose it is only natural.

21 June 1941.
We have enjoyed a cool wind which is very welcome after the heat of the harbour.

When we first sailed into the tropics, windsails were erected. These were great canvas affairs consisting of long sausages about three feet in diameter, suspended vertically from the rigging, down into the holds. At the top of each sausage a large triangular canvas on each side acted as catchment area, thus scooping the maximum amount of wind into the sausage. This nice clean fresh air was poured downwards into the holds, thus producing a sort of Heath Robinson cooling system.

22 June 1941.
Guard again, otherwise all is the same. A rumour has circulated the ship that Russia has declared war on Germany. My collection of books is extending rapidly; I have acquired two today. I have lost my razor, (a Wilkinson's strop, so rather special).

23 June 1941.
I slept on deck last night, but was almost blown away in the process. For guard I had the windiest post, so I felt rather like a windmill. I regret to say that while on guard, I must have fallen asleep because the time passed much too quickly.

Had I been found asleep, I should probably have been given another duty. Luck was in.

24 June 1941.
A storm is brewing so for the next few days we shall be in for a tossing. There has been a strong wind ever since we left port but we have not felt the effects so far. This afternoon, Wing Commander Tanner (OC troops) talked to us about the next port of call – Durban. We shall be allowed ashore from 1 o'clock to 12. He also said that our destination is Egypt.

My memory is of a total absence of officers in spite of the fact that there were about 300 aboard. No doubt I have forgotten, but I cannot remember much effort being taken to ease the strain of our confinement. OC troops talk was welcome.

25 June 1941.
It has been much cooler today. I had a very comfortable night on deck. The storm has arrived.

To a reader of the present generation, 'a ship' is, typically, a cross channel ferry. The *Eastern Prince* bore little relationship to such a vessel – apart from its general shape! It smelt of the sea, it had plank, caulked decks which were scrubbed every morning by the crew – trousers rolled up and bare feet – or am I thinking of films! One knew one was at sea, and Masefield caught the flavour of it even though we were a couple of decades later.

26 June 1941.
Three days rest then guard again today. The storm has been blowing up all day, and it is now nearly as rough as in the North Atlantic. Everyone says it will be rougher round the Cape, but I don't mind, – I like it. I have found my razor; some kind person had taken it to the orderly room. While on guard, the Wing Commander (OC Troops) came round and spoke to me – he is very nice.

Lost razor returned. An honest lot.
Footwear throughout the voyage was issue type plimsolls, to protect the wooden deck.

27 June 1941.
The storm is becoming very severe. I went along to the bow a few

times during the day. Spray was breaking over the ship so one had to look out; I was almost caught two or three times but just managed to steer clear. Bridge has been the main occupation for the rest of the day.

28 June 1941.
The storm has reached its peak. While at boat stations, we saw the *Empress of Japan* put her bow right under, so that water was then streaming off the bridge for at least half a minute afterwards.

This was the first occasion when our good ship played her trump card. The noise of all noises, and quake of all quakes. We were bowling along into the teeth of the gale, the bow deep into the waves one minute, then soaring sky high the next. Unbeknown to us landlubbers, the flat of the hull rose clear of the water, then it plunged downwards into the next wave, the flat hitting the ocean with an almighty crash, shaking the vessel from stem to stern. Our immediate reaction was that we had been torpedoed. (To ensure maximum effect, this performance should be scheduled for the small hours).

Another fascinating noise is produced at the other end of the ship. In the same sea, the stern copies the bow, so that from time to time, the former emerges from the water. As this is the business end, the screws suddenly find that they are no longer in water; they increase their speed and thrash the air, making a lot of hoo-ha in the process.

29 June 1941.
The storm has blown itself out. I am rather disappointed, but one cannot expect it to go on for ever, and anyway some people don't like it much. In the evening we went up on deck for an hour and enjoyed the stars. Am not sure which is the Southern Cross.

Afterwards, we went to the concert. Had to stand all the time, but very enjoyable.

30 June 1941.
On guard again, but on the whole a good thing – something to do. It was announced today that we shall call at Capetown tomorrow instead of Durban, and probably stay there for about a week. Because of this, the water has been on all day, so that we have been able to do our washing; I had a lot to get through. I am glad it will be Capetown, I have always wanted to visit there rather than other African towns.

We were surrounded by water, but what about the fresh variety? The vessel was not designed to carry so many passengers, so fresh water was in short supply. Salt water showers had been installed on deck, and these were always available, but fresh water was turned on for only an hour morning and evening. Within this time scale, one had to wash and do one's laundry.

1 July 1941.
It has been my day for performing the chores, and a disagreeable affair too. After coming off guard at 9 o'clock I had to scour everything for an inspection. No sooner was that finished than there was lunch to do.

Capetown. We first sighted some hills just after 9 am. Six ships (including ours) broke off from the main convoy which continues to Durban. By 11, we could see the hills fairly clearly; they were steep cliffs. As we came nearer they took definite shape, and were bare and barren at that. The piece of coastline directly in front of us was a long line of hills with a sort of sentinel at each end. Soon, the town became visible, but not what I had expected. The buildings were all built of yellow stone and had red roofs. One or two large buildings stood out more than the others, especially round the docks. The whole place was completely dominated by Table Mountain which gave a sort of predominating magnificence, and at the same time a feeling of insignificance to the town. The mountain itself had a very steep face on the seaward side and there was no vegetation to soften its hardness. However on closer inspection, some deciduous trees were visible.

By 3 o'clock we were lying in the bay opposite the dock. Various vessels were at anchor including two American ships. When I came on deck after tea, I discovered that we had come alongside. Natives were scrambling for pennies thrown down to them. Rumour quickly spread that we would be allowed ashore at 7, so there was a general scramble to get changed. About 6 o'clock when chaos was greatest, what should happen? The lights went out for about 15 minutes. I went on deck where – low and behold – THE SHIP WAS FLOODLIT, AND THE WHOLE TOWN A BLAZE OF LIGHTS. I then realised how much we missed lights in England. The place was like a million twinkling stars and an absolute joy.

By now there was general agitation about going ashore, then we were told that only odd number mess tables would be allowed to go. I always seem to be unlucky. To drown our sorrows we made a four at bridge, and played on deck beneath the flood-lighting. I decided to sleep on deck; however by morning the idea had not been so good. It was cold, and I saw in the paper that Kimberley had had its first fall of snow for twenty-five years. No wonder it was cold.

Chapter 6

AT SEA – TO SUEZ

Cape Town + Table Mountain

Capetown. By contrast with Britain in 1941, this was a place of peace and plenty. No rationing, no blackout, no bombing; so different from Liverpool four weeks before. It was not surprising that we revelled in it.

2 July 1941.

The ship was floodlit all night, so it never got dark. We were given our shore passes at about 12 o'clock which created great excitement below deck. We queued up for half an hour to get off, then it was grand to feel solid earth under foot after four weeks at sea. A lorry gave us a lift to the dock gates. Just outside, a kiosk offered information on things to do; they included a tour of the countryside followed by a dance, but I wanted to see the town.

The town is built in squares, so it is easy to find one's way around. Buildings are modern, and there is a good view up the main street with the railway station on the left. At the top, an attractive avenue has the Houses of Parliament on the left and a park on the right. Being mid-winter, plants were not in bloom, but squirrels with 'misty' tails were everywhere – pretty things. I did a bit of shopping and in the process lost my companion, so wandered on alone. I went up the hill at the seaward end of the town and admired the city from above. I talked to a gunner who was born in Croydon, but had lived here all his life. He warned me not to take photographs. I stayed up there watching the lights come on in the town. I had tea at the YMCA and better still – a bath.

I bought some postcards and talked to the proprietor of the shop for about half an hour: he invited me in any time I liked. The inhabitants of Capetown are the most friendly people I have ever known. It is almost impossible to walk about without someone coming up and offering assistance. Also, there is less class distinction than in Britain: other ranks are not refused admittance into hotels.

A bath: seventh heaven, as every serviceman will know. The salt-water showers on the ship were not the same as a fresh-water bath.

The hospitality of the South Africans amazed us all. After our first return from being ashore we compared notes. Not one of us had been ignored by the people of Capetown. Many had been taken for long drives up country, and into peoples' homes to share their lives for a few brief hours. Some were given presents, and the South Africans wanted to know how Britain was coping under war conditions. And to think that we were just one ship-load to be given this treatment; I have no doubt that every troop-ship that put into Capetown, Durban or Port Elizabeth received an equal welcome. What a people.

Inevitably, food on the ship left a lot to be desired, so that a change of diet in ration-free Capetown offered one long gobble. We discovered oranges. Large luscious 'Outspans'. Every airman returning to the ship was loaded with oranges, ranging from a paper bagful to a mini-sack. They kept us going for quite a long time after leaving port.

3 July 1941.
I have been on shore picket today. We had to fall in at 1.45, and from there we marched into the city to arrive at 3 o'clock. Difficult to believe it took so long. On arrival at The Square, we were detailed to go into Capetown with an MP (Military Policeman), and to wander round enforcing order. The MP was rather young and very keen; he seemed to take a delight in telling people to take their hands out of their pockets. Our beat lay around the centre of the town; we just wandered from one street to another until we felt hungry. A Baptist church gave us free tea. Later, an officer told us our assistance was needed. A man (serviceman?) was very drunk, bellowing and yelling. Eventually, he was taken away in a police van. More food, then we were dismissed at 8.10 and a hateful job was over. I then went to the cinema with Laurie, and got back to the boat at 1 a.m. after coffee and biscuits. I took some fruit back to the ship.

This business of pickets was an on-going duty for troops stationed near a town. Order had to be kept, and drink was available. By 10 p.m. there were likely to be incidents. RAF and Army Military Policemen formed the nucleus of these order-keeping patrols, but because they were too few in number, they were augmented by additional manpower from local units. The Capetown picket was the first of many that came my way. I cannot pretend that I enjoyed them.

4 July 1941.

It was a lovely morning so we decided to make for the top of Table Mountain. However, it was announced during the morning that the CO would inspect our deck, with the result that we were not off the boat until 2 p.m. We beetled into town and went to find out about transport to the lower (cable car) station. It was frequent, so no need for agitation. We had been told about a book shop where every member of the forces was given one free book. We went there, and my choice was *Nanking Road* by Viki Baum. Further diversions, and we reached the bottom of the mountain by 5.30, getting to the top by 6.30. I had never been in a cable car before. We came to the upper station just as the sun was setting, and the view was absolutely magnificent. There was slight haze but not enough to matter. Capetown lay a mile below us and looked exactly like a map. One could identify all the main streets and buildings. We didn't leave the top until after dark so that we had the most wonderful panoramic view of the lights.

We were not allowed ashore in the mornings. Considering that we had been cooped up in the vessel for so long, this was frustrating, but we had to put up with it. To be fair, we were allowed to return to the ship as late as 1 a.m. which was more than reasonable, but many of us would have preferred an earlier departure to a late return.

In all seriousness, had there been more time, one or two of us would have liked to climb Table Mountain on foot. As it was, we had to make do with the cable car. This was my first mountain and set the pattern for many more, either on foot or by whatever transport was offered. Our own Ben Nevis etc. then Shamsan in Aden, Brinchang in Malaya, The Peak in Hongkong and Penang, the Banihal Pass and Lake Gangerbal (12,500 ft) below Mount Harmoukh in Kashmir, not to mention all the highest passes in France by car, with occasional excursions on foot to the tops of the lesser peaks (Tete de la Maye at 2,519 metres in the Ecrins National Park, and others). A wonderful world up there, and to stand on the top, after a long climb, gives a tremendous sense of achievement. I can recommend it to anyone.

The book shop was a very good example of the kindness of the South African people, and the free book was an opportunity not to be missed. It was true, and my choice of *Nanking Road* was a good one. Before leaving the shop, I was asked the name and address of my next of kin. Subsequently, my mother told me that she had received a letter from the shop, assuring her that I had passed through, and that I was fit and well. What more could one ask of a people?

5 July 1941.
During breakfast, an NCO came down and called the roll. We gathered that we should not be going ashore again. We left the quay at 1 o'clock and by 2 p.m. we were out in the harbour and sailing away, leaving only a memory of three very enjoyable days. It was most noticeable that everyone was very quiet, hardly anyone saying anything. We were still within sight of the peninsular when the sun set. So far it is very calm, not what we expected round the Cape. I remembered that from the top of the mountain, the waves looked so small, and seemed to crawl. Now we were amongst them.

6 July 1941.
Dawn showed that we were out of sight of land, travelling south easterly. During the day we gradually veered towards the north east, which became our course. Everyone has been feeling very depressed, and I must admit that I am as well. It struck me during the evening that if Russia is defeated, which seems likely, then there isn't much

chance of winning the war. If that happens all our money will go unless we have land. I wish Mother could buy some.

A great event: I got out a most complicated 'patience'!

I find no mention in my diary of the *Queen Mary* and *Queen Elizabeth*. Shortly after leaving Capetown, I can remember that we saw a large vessel on the horizon which was identified as one of the two Queens. These two ships were used to bring Australian and New Zealand troops to Europe before they transported thousands of GIs across the Atlantic. The sighting added spice to life.

7 July 1941.

I started to write a letter home in case we call in at Durban, but a notice on DROs told us not to mention Capetown in correspondence. This seems ridiculous; I so wanted to tell my mother about Table Mountain and all the rest of it.

The sea is so calm, and no sign of a monsoon. How tempting to jump in. After dark, I went on deck for an hour and watched the moon on the water. Absolutely beautiful.

Once we were in the tropics the hours of darkness had lengthened and the smokers in our company were penalised. For obvious reasons there was no smoking below deck, but additionally no smoking was allowed on deck after dark. Laughable though it may seem, a lot of lighted cigarettes could lead to a ship being sunk. Another aspect of security at sea, of which I was not aware at the time, was the dumping of garbage. Flotsam could tell tales, and I'm told that all rubbish from all ships at sea was dumped overboard at the same time each day – midday I believe.

8 July 1941.
Guard again today, on the port deck. A rough sea has been coming up since morning. The increase in swell was quite visible during my two hours on duty. It is almost as rough as it is in the Atlantic.

A spirit of discontent is running through the ship, and I shan't be surprised if there is trouble shortly. Everyone is feeling pretty fed up after five weeks at sea, and they are finding things to grumble about, especially the food and canteen. Also, the officers are detested, which is understandable when one considers the difference in treatment between officers and men.

Yes, we hated the officers. The situation was handled badly; I thought so at the time, but now, with hindsight, I cannot understand why officers were not detailed off at the beginning of the voyage to look after each mess deck. By doing so, the men would have had regular contact with the officers, and there would have been feedback to OC troops. Half an hour spent informally by an officer down there in the hold talking to the men would have made all the difference in the world. Actually, OC Troops himself was a delightful, understanding man, but perhaps a bit old for the job. Also, this was his first voyage as an OC Troops, so no doubt he learned from it, and subsequent organisation was better. I will have more to say about man management in the RAF in due course.

9 July 1941.
By morning the storm had completely abated, but we were going round in circles. I learned that we were waiting for a convoy to join us from Durban. Washing-up day on the mess deck; not as bad as some.

Washing-up was clearing away the debris of meals. Not nice.

10 July 1941.
In the afternoon, the CO gave us a little talk on insects, and Egypt in general; it seems pretty certain that we are going there. The CO is much more understanding than the rest of the officers on board. He quite casually brought up the subject of canteen prices, and explained them.

The sea is often calm, but I have never seen it as it was tonight. The only cloud was to the west, so that it was pale blue, tinged with red; the water was exactly like a millpond without a ripple. It was the palest possible blue with streaks of gold from the setting sun. With the ships sailing gently forward it was one of the most beautiful scenes I have ever seen.

11 July 1941.
The clock went forward during the night, but some people didn't know until the evening! An industrious day, writing letters and doing laundry.

We had to be self-sufficient. With very restricted fresh water, laundry was a problem; the answer was to wear as little as possible which was easier once we were into the tropics.

12 July 1941.
Guard duty again, but quite enjoyable, basking in the sun on deck watching for submarines. During the afternoon, I turned tailor and sewed up my trousers.

Submarine guard was the best, up on the top deck, keeping a look out.

I wonder if I would have seen a submarine had there been one.

Sewing up trousers. We had been issued with tropical kit in the UK, but inevitably it was not the sort worn in the tropics. The trousers were a masterpiece: very baggy, half-length. The idea was to wear them turned down (to calf length) at night, and turned up during the day, held up by buttons. We resorted to sewing them up permanently, or cutting them off. Another prize item was the solar topi, a great heavy thing which was replaced by the light-weight pith helmet when we arrived in Egypt.

12 to 15 July 1941.
Top deck, sunbathing, writing letters, reading, playing bridge. During the last two days the RAF has started issuing us with two bottles of lemonade per day – almost undrinkable.

The lemonade was no doubt to guarantee our fluid intake now that we were into really hot weather.

16 July 1941.
At 2 a.m. I had to evacuate my bed hastily to visit the lavatory. Continued all night and I reported sick at 8 a.m. I was excused guard, but at 1 p.m. I was hauled down for it. While on guard, I was ticked off by 'Walrus' for sitting down; told him why, but he said he wanted no barrack-room lawyer stunts from me. Laurie volunteered to do my night shift.

No malingering.

17 July 1941.
At last I have realised why we appear to be travelling so slowly. The sea has been running from our rear ever since we turned north. Pre-

vailing winds, according to the geography book, do exist after all. Nothing like practical experience to improve one's understanding.

18 July 1941.
At 1.05 p.m. precisely, half the convoy broke away to the east – for India, leaving us to travel north-west. This changed to north in the evening so we are entering the Gulf of Aden.

19 July 1941.
A strong wind during the night, giving us a considerable roll. When the wind dropped, it left an absolutely calm sea and frightful heat – the worst to date. Sighted British Somaliland.

20 July 1941.
Guard again. Quite enjoyable, watching the flying fish.

21 July 1941.
We sighted land first thing this morning and were anchored by 9 a.m. We approached from the west – we always seem to overshoot. Aden is more or less what I expected, being quite barren. It is built on the side of an absolutely rocky, bare mountain. This must throw tremendous heat onto the town. The mountain is not as high or precipitous as Table Mountain but has the same effect of dwarfing the town, which is not as antiquated as I expected. We can see two churches and a hotel – The Crescent. There are only a few trees, but no sign of other natural vegetation. The ships anchor in the bay, and passengers go ashore by boat. For refuelling, we have been connected to a buoy, labelled Iranian Oil, some 50 yards from the shore. I wonder if Aden is supplied by pipe across Arabia? Natives came round the ship selling their wares – mostly melons. I wonder where

they grow them; we bought one. The natives seem a better type than at Freetown. The water was on, so I have done all my laundry; very necessary.

It so happens that I spent ten days in Aden in the transit camp eighteen months later on my way to India. Then we spent two years there as a family in the late 1950s. It was a good station, but desperately hot and humid from May until September (which included this period when we sat in the harbour). The winter is like a good English summer. There is indeed no shortage of water; it comes from the hinterland where mountains rising to about 8,000 feet have the rainfall – and where the melons come from.

22 July 1941.
Refuelling was finished and we moved out into the bay at 8 a.m. to allow another ship in. I thought we were leaving port but was wrong. The bay has proved just as hot as close inshore in spite of slightly more breeze. This afternoon we were told to get our packing done, but it was so hot in the hold that I gave up.

23 July 1941.
If we are going to disembark (in Egypt) on Sunday, as rumoured, we had better get a move on. All the ships have finished refuelling but we stay at anchor. There have been a lot of fatigues during the day, but I have escaped them. The main job has been piling up the deep-sea kit bags, which we are told we shall have to carry ashore ourselves.

The reason for the long delay was that we were waiting to form a convoy. Shortly before this, the Canal Zone had been bombed by the

Italians and the SS *Georgic* had been a victim. A 'lucky' bomb penetrated a hatch while she was at anchor at Port Teufik, and she burned out. The wreck was there for us to see when we arrived. As a result of this bombing, convoys were formed for the trip up the Red Sea.

24 July 1941.
Still no movement away from this oven. We just lie and roast. The NAAFI has run out of oranges. There are plenty of apples, but they are not very good and do not quench the thirst.

25 July 1941.
Guard in No. 5 hold and 'a little hot' at 97 degrees, though it felt much more. While down there I got into conversation with another lad from St Eval. It makes a good change to find somebody else to talk to; I have been with the same company all the time so far, and I have got frightfully tired of them by now.

I have tried not to bore my readers with a precise record of day-to-day activities. I have singled out only items of general interest. However, my readers may wonder how we passed the time, day after day. Apart from daily muster parade, guards, fatigues and meal times, we had the rest of the days to ourselves. The company we kept was more or less confined to our own mess deck, and we formed cliques with little cross-fertilisation. My own clique originated from lads I had been with at Halton and St Eval, and I suppose like sifted with like. No doubt another Erk's report of this journey would be quite different. My lot were quiet and serious. There were a lot more boisterous elements around, but we went our own way and did not mix with them. I have already mentioned bridge, and this was our clique's main occupation. Enough of us knew the game to make a four at any time, and spend quite a few hours 'at the table' – on the deck!

– every day. We talked. I spent many hours at the rail watching the sea. Apart from that, my refuge was reading, and I was always content to put my nose into a book. The hours passed, and the days passed to become weeks, with no responsibilities or *raison d'être* – no doubt, much the same as for a prisoner in a jail.

26 July 1941.
Still no sign of departure. There are dozens of rumours as to why we are stuck here; and there is one that we are going ashore tomorrow. I doubt it. Tonight, I feel that I simply hate the RAF and everything and everyone to do with it, especially the foul language; I can't understand why everything has to be described by such lewd adjectives.

27 July 1941.
Some time ago, I suggested that if conditions remain as they are, something would happen. This evening it has. On DROs today 'other ranks' were told that they could listen to a concert through the lounge windows. This insult was like a spark. At 8.30 when the concert started, a mob was on the deck. They started shouting and causing a disturbance. After half an hour, a WO came out and did some bargaining which ended in an agreement that the CO would speak to us at 11.15 tomorrow. I can't quite decide how I feel about it. It seems rather stupid to have a riot just before we are likely to go ashore; we shall probably not be allowed to go. As for the reasons for the rioting, there are certainly plenty of complaints about our present conditions. However, when it comes to the point, there are a good many in the ranks who have no cause to grumble; after all, the things which I feel and grumble about are not the things most of the men are used to, but I accept it. I do

think the officers might try to live with the men a bit more; it would make us feel less like vermin.

This morning, it was announced that 3 men from each mess table could go ashore. Nothing came of it, which added to the discontent.

For a short time, the scene was quite ugly. Fire-hoses were trained into the saloon. They were not turned on, but the threat was by no means idle.

Are these the words of a pampered brat? At this distance I can view them dispassionately. We all come from different backgrounds, and mine was that of stepson of a retired army colonel, brought up in the country, with access to all the big houses where servants and silver were on tap. My standards were therefore high in speech, behaviour and conduct. I was also used to an above average standard of cooking. Without any disrespect to my companions, I believe I was experiencing a greater reduction in living standards than almost anyone else on that ship. If they had cause to complain, then my cause was that much greater. But I didn't. I accepted the situation. No doubt the extreme discipline I had been subjected to since coming into the orbit of my stepfather had something to do with it. I would go so far as to say that extreme discipline produces either an aggressive kicker against the traces, or a more subtle character, who bends with the wind, but does not break. This latter was my doctrine, and it served me in good stead under these shipboard conditions. The difference in our standards can most obviously be summed up in the language, about which I commented earlier. On that ship, everything from a tea mug onwards indulged in permanent copulation. We were not short of blasting at home, but rude words were not included. One would like to think – quite mistakenly – that we all aspire to being a gentleman. Being a gentleman has nothing to do with birth. The highest in the land can be the worst self-seeking cad – un-gentleman! – and we can, all of us, name a few, while the most humble man can be a perfect gentleman. I am still old-fashioned enough to believe that 'manners maketh man', and that starts with speech.

28 July 1941.
We have been in Aden for a week, and on board for 8 weeks. More than enough for anyone. The CO spoke to us as agreed. He was nothing like as severe as I expected. He gave us a resumé of the voyage, and said it was only a bloody ship if we chose to make it one. He then told us to ask questions, and put forward ideas. This was done; I could not hear a word of it, but everyone ended up feeling appeased. We were also told that after lunch we would be going inshore to re-water, and while there, we would be allowed ashore. This actually happened.

I learned that this is Steamer Point. Aden town is five miles away. It is not as bad as I expected. All the bazaar shops are strung along the main street. Being native shops, one has to bargain for half an hour before a reasonable price is agreed. I only bought stamps and postcards; it is too difficult to carry anything big on the ship. I don't like bargaining, but I suppose I shall have to get used to it. We went ashore by launch, so we saw for the first time our noble ship *Eastern Prince* as others see her, and she carries herself off very well. It is such a pity that she is so crowded inside.

The old town of Aden bakes in the sun in a corner of the crater, immediately behind a half-mile sandy shore. To the rear, it is completely surrounded by the lip of the crater, rising to 2,000 feet at its highest point. There are only two ways into the town: firstly from the sea level sandy isthmus of Khormaksar at the north-east where the coastal rock has been blasted away to make a road; and secondly through a man-made gap at the top of a narrow pass, spanned by a hundred-year-old fortified bridge. Alas, since our departure, the bridge has been destroyed to make room for a dual carriageway.

During my two year tour in Aden, I made my first climb to the top of Shamsan from the furthest point beyond Crater Town, where the lip of the crater descends precipitously into the ocean. My army driver dropped me and I then made my way across the upper reaches of the crater. It was an eerie experience. This no-man's-land appeared to be divided into little territories, each guarded by a pie-dog, and each baying to the moon. Halfway across I encountered a wild-eyed Arab who wanted money – I did not surrender my wallet, but I wondered what I had let myself in for.

Later when I took my wife up Shamsan, we went by the conventional route, leading from the top of the pass.

Aden Crater Town.

79

30 July 1941.

After yesterday, it has been the same as any other day; I woke this morning to find that we were just moving out of port. The *Castle* ship is with us. After lunch we passed a number of islands. There was a settlement of some sort on one of them, (Perrin Island); just a few stone buildings with an oil reservoir. If Aden was bad, I dare not think what it would be like here. A very strong wind has been increasing since 3 p.m. I am glad we are not in the desert, having sand in our faces.

30 July – 2 August 1941.

Either a strong wind, or the sea as calm as a mill pond. The heat has been appalling – stuffy hot and breathless. Washing-up in the hold was awful. As we approached Suez we had a practice in case of air attack. There is land on both sides, much the same as Aden. I am dreading three years in this place.

3 August 1941.

The voyage has ended at last. It has not been too bad, and from subsequent conversations, other ships seem to have been worse. At first sight, Egypt looks as though it will be worse.

We had reveille at 5 a.m, then after general clean-up of the ship, we waited about on deck with all our kit until 11 a.m. At last we went ashore in ferries, and waited a further 1½ hours for transport to take us to the RAF Pool camp.

And so we arrived at our destination nine weeks after our departure from Liverpool. To travel 3,000 miles, we had crossed some 15,000 miles of ocean (say fifteen knots a day for seven weeks actual sailing time). 1,500 of us were cooped up in 11,000 tons of steel. Some fleeting moments were unforgettable – first sight of land in the tropics at Freetown, Capetown and Table Mountain; riding the Atlantic at the bow of the ship in the storm; the still beauty of the Indian Ocean. Against that, the conditions under which we lived were trying, to say the least. The nearest comparison I can make is with a cross-channel ferry, at peak hour, but with only the most basic facilities – wash house, latrine, mess deck. No tables, no chairs, no luxuries of any sort. No alcohol. You, my reader, are reading these words today. Think back sixty-two days. What were you doing then? From that moment until this, is the length of time that we spent on SS *Eastern Prince*. We had just four half-days ashore. During the whole of that time it was possible to distance oneself by no more than ten feet – no FIVE feet – from one's companions. Nine uninterrupted weeks of close proximity to one's fellow beings. Inevitably it was a strain, and dare I say, more so for a country lad who, even at the best of times, was not at ease in the company of others. What a good thing he had developed a mental suit of armour to protect himself.

This is not a whinge; it did no harm, and in the long run, made me a better officer when handling the men under my command.

Chapter 7

BOMBS AWAY

A Blenheim with opt.

We had arrived in the land of the Pharaohs. Because Port Teufik did not have a wharf, we came ashore by tender. Fortunately, there was a good bund with trees so that we were able to sit in the shade. We were given tea and buns, and an officer told us with glee that we were just in time for the battle of the Middle East. What an encouraging thought when we had hardly found our land legs!

After over an hour's wait, lorries arrived to take us to the RAF Pool Camp. This was some thirty miles to the north. We clambered into the vehicles with our kit and were then bowled along a road which followed a railway line across miles of sand. Following the whim of some eccentric, the road ran on one side of the track, then for no apparent reason crossed over to the other side. The crossing points were protected by sort of sheep hurdles. Sitting crammed into the back of the lorry – I cannot remember if it had a canvas top or not – we could feel the heat and dust blowing up into our faces.

Arriving at the camp, we were dumped by the road, then had to find a space in a tent for the night. Tea: there was a queue miles long outside a cook-house so we had no alternative but to stand and wait. We were surprised to find the food rather better than expected.

We were covered with dust from the journey and longed for a bath, but not a bit of it; there was only one tap for washing. The answer was to go down to the Bitter Lake and have a bathe; not the same thing at all in such salty water, but at least it was warm and wet and better than nothing. While bathing we could see the wrecks of some vessels sticking out of the water. By the time we had finished bathing the sun had gone down so we made our way back to the camp in the fast gathering darkness. On the way we had our first sight of a native village. Stalls and hubbub, illuminated by paraffin lamps and pressure lamps. How did this compare with the High Street? Where were World Store and Woolworths, Boots and Burtons? We bought a melon in exchange for three cigarettes, and consumed this before we turned in for the night.

I slept well; after all, lying on sand was softer than a wooden deck. It was unexpectedly cool first thing, when we went on parade at 7.45. To our astonishment our postings were read out. Things in the RAF had never happened as fast as that before; however there had to be a first time. In spite of this early morning manifestation, we had to hang about all day and did not depart the Pool Camp until 4 p.m. A drive of about one and a half hours brought us to our new station, 108 Maintenance Unit at Abu Suier, a few miles to the west of Ismailia.

Here, I should explain the purpose of a Maintenance Unit. Its role is geared into the maintenance schedule of aircraft. The serviceability of an aircraft is dependent upon its maintenance schedule, and every aircraft has one. Working up from the bottom, there is a simple inspection after every flight, however short; this includes the checking of all working controls. Thereafter, inspections take place after a set number of flying hours, say 50, then 100, and so on. Each inspection is more complex than the last, and all are carried out by the regular maintenance crew on the operational airfield. After an aircraft has flown a greater number of hours it is subjected to a major overhaul. This involves a lot of dismantling, checking of individual parts and replacement of any parts suspected of being faulty. This work is time-consuming, and often requires specialist equipment; it is therefore better performed away from the operational airfield. Consequently, the machine is flown to a base workshop, which is the Maintenance Unit. Such a place was 108 MU.

Abu Suier was a peace-time station. It was therefore well appointed. Buildings were permanent structures, there were hangars to work in. Good hutted accommodation, messing facilities, YMCA canteens and all mod. cons. Unfortunately because of the excess numbers of airmen in camp, we were put into tents, but that was just bad luck. The roads ran through avenues of trees (eucalyptus) and there was grass, carefully tended by the native Egyptian labour. My first impression was 'jolly good, this will suit me for as long as I am in the Middle East'. Furthermore the first midday meal was excellent – salmon, tomato and cucumber.

Introduction to the station on the first morning included a number of little chats by officers and WOs, telling us all the do's and don'ts. Then to work in the afternoon.

There had been a bit of bombing of the area before we arrived with the result that all personnel not actually on duty were sent out into the desert to sleep at an old camp area, known as Q Camp. This meant setting out on foot across two (did my diary exaggerate?) miles of sand, carrying our bedding.

Working conditions in the hangars were good; they were free from dust and were cool, though they warmed up a bit in the afternoons. Working outside was a different story, particularly inside a plane. I was ordered to join a crew under the command of a corporal, with the task of changing a bulkhead. Oh what a lot of nuts and bolts!

The working day was long. We returned to camp from the desert at 5.30 a.m. and went to work immediately after breakfast. Two hours off in the middle of the day for midday meal and a short rest, then on again in the afternoon to finish at 5 p.m. prior to going out to dispersal at 6.30. Sundays started an hour later and we only worked in the morning. With luck we had Saturday afternoons off, and I went into Ismailia on one of them.

In order to put these events into the correct time-scale, I think it advisable, at this stage, to do a short resumé of the state of the war in the Middle East. It was now the late summer of 1941. At the beginning of the year General Wavell's army (prior to 8th Army time) had advanced into Cyrenaica and had captured Benghazi. Thousands of Italian prisoners of war had been taken, and were being used by the military for miscellaneous tasks. In February, General Rommel had arrived, and by the summer, his presence had been felt. All the territory taken earlier in the year had been lost and Tobruk was surrounded. In June, General Wavell was replaced by General Auchinleck, and both sides were having a pause to build up strength for a push in the late autumn. The Balkans had been overrun, and Crete evacuated; many of the refugees arrived in Egypt (including an old family friend from Dorset, who had got away from Crete in a rowing boat). Nearly another year was to pass before the Afrika Corps was poised on the outskirts of the Delta.

12 August 1941.

Things are becoming distinctly active. During the night there was an air-raid which, although not very heavy, was extremely profitable to Jerry. About 36 bombs were dropped and yet those few caused a tremendous amount of damage. There must be a 5th columnist at work. A train at the station was hit as well, but that was because it showed its lights – stupid idiots. I was expecting a raid because I had heard the gunners being given their orders: however it didn't come until 4 a.m. when I was woken up by the Bofort firing at an aircraft. The gunner was cursed severely for giving away his position.

As soon as the bombs started to fall, nearly everyone near me picked up his bed and rushed to the other side of the camp. They are fools, they are just as likely to be hit over there as here. I stayed put, but I must admit that I did not particularly like being by myself. In the morning, we found trees down and water everywhere. The fires were more or less out by 7 a.m. We spent most of the day picking up broken glass.

This first major raid on the Station caused a re-think about dispersal. The area we were using was quite close to the camp so a new place was found further away. There were some old huts, devoid of furniture and with holes in the rooves, but it was luxury after the last place. We travelled out and back by transport, and we felt like something out of a Hollywood film, trekking across the desert, with clouds of dust flying.

Having arrived out there, I would wander out to a ridge where the sand was completely clean and virgin; so different from the filthy stuff around the camp. The setting sun would shed a glorious red light over the sand. One could not ask for better. It was close to full moon, and almost as bright as day with the light reflected off the sand. On one occasion I found a corporal out there writing a poem. He had chosen the ideal place to do it.

13 August 1941.
Another raid during the night, but not as harmful as the last. The ack-ack barrage improved a lot and the enemy were kept at bay.

Even so, they managed to blow up a hangar, plus one or two other things.

Wogs*, who had all cleared off yesterday, returned today. I am on guard tonight, and not looking forward to it.

14 August 1941.
Luck held. We were not raided, but a neighbouring camp had the hell of a plastering. From 3 a.m. we spent the night in the shelter.

There was a regular fire-fighting unit on Station strength, but it was not designed to deal with fires of this magnitude; it was therefore augmented by fire pickets. All the lads on Station took their turn, though I can find no reference to such a duty in my diary. I can only assume that I was on duty on a non-raid night. These pickets slept at the nearby Q camp so that they were only on Station when actually fighting fires.

Another duty we had to do was 'Dispersal Party'. This involved taking all the aircraft at the end of the day and dotting them about the aerodrome at a distance from one another, thus minimising bomb damage. We used a towing tractor for this but, being a non-driver, I was just an odd body securing chocks and things like that. On at least one occasion we finished after the lorries had gone out to dispersal, so that I bedded down in camp. It so happened that there were no raids on those nights.

On 15 August I received my first communication from home. It was only a postcard, posted on the 15 July, and told me there were ten letters on the way. The great thing was that it put me in touch again. I had sent a cablegram when I first arrived, and had been told that it should take

---

* I am faced with a problem. Should I be politically correct or honest? I have decided that, because I am writing about 1941, I should use the word of the period however much that might appal the present-day reader. Am I now in the dog house?

only three to four days to get to England.

There was pressure on us to work faster, and on Saturday 23 August, we were told that we could not have the afternoon off; however our Sergeant stood up for us and told the officer that we had little enough time to ourselves without removing Saturday afternoon. The officer relented! What did I do with the time? Read and wrote letters. Shortly after this, it was agreed that we could stop work at 4.30 to give us a few more minutes before going out to dispersal. In the interim we had to squeeze in queuing for tea, washing and general titivation, so there was not much spare time. Another snag, of course, was lack of lights out at dispersal. From about 6.30 onwards we were in darkness.

Rumours were flying about that we were going to move. Some of the men had left, and space was available in the permanent accommodation, so I claimed a place. Even though I did not sleep in it, it was wonderful to have a locker, fans and no sand underfoot. When I was manhandling my kit from tent to billet, a very small wog came and carried my suitcase (which I had bought in Ismailia) for me. I gave him one piastre. I went to wash, and when I returned, he had cleaned my boots for me. A taste of being an effendi for one gorgeous minute!

2 September 1941.

There wasn't a raid last night. I shall be on guard tomorrow night, and I would quite like to be in a raid. I have watched them long enough.

The spirit in camp is very much lacking. It was put into words this evening by a Corporal when dispersing aircraft. 'Put the . . . thing in line with those two and hope to God he drops a bomb on them.' He wasn't joking, and what's more, everyone feels the same, including me – to a certain extent. It wouldn't be so bad if it weren't for the heat which is overpowering in the afternoons.

Do I see eyebrows being raised at this revelation? Hold on a moment – the British Tommy (excuse me, RAF, but we were Tommies in blue) was always outspoken, and his words should not be taken at face value. Things on Station were not quite as good as they might have been for a number of reasons, so don't blame him too much.

We have heard praise many, many times by bomber and fighter crews of their maintenance crews. Then why the difference in a Maintenance Unit? The short answer is because of lack of allegiance. In an operational unit, whether it be Army, RAF or Navy, every man knows that, whatever his job, the success of the whole team depends upon his own contribution. The bomber crew could not do its job if the fitters failed to look after the aircraft properly, and the aircraft takes on the personality of the crew who fly it. It is no longer an inanimate object without a pilot. It is no longer one of hundreds of aircraft, it is THE aircraft, the only one. Both crews meld together into one crew, and the bond works both ways.

Work in a Maintenance Unit is different. Here the aircraft is just one of those hundreds, a heap of metal without a soul, so why should the fitter owe it special allegiance? And the fitters working companions are a polyglot lot, here today and gone tomorrow to another place. They are individual tradesmen with their own interests uppermost in their minds. A few of them may be teams and know one another quite well, but then RHB and others are thrust into their midst and cohesion is lost. No doubt the permanent cadre of the Station, the Officers Mess and the Senior NCOs Mess had a togetherness, but this did not stretch down to the miscellaneous body of Erks. Every serviceman knows this, including our offending corporal. Had he been in an operational unit his reaction would have been quite different. Under the circumstances, his comment was not unreasonable. Seeking an interpretation for the benefit of the traveller on that omnibus in south-west London, I would suggest that it is the same as the matriarchal feeling Mum has for the rest of the family.

4 September 1941.

The day before yesterday I expressed a wish for a raid while on guard duty. This is exactly what happened. I was on second relief and due to go on at the gate at 9 p.m. However, at 8.45, the warning sounded, and I was sent out to reinforce the other sentry. We had been there about half an hour, hearing aircraft flying overhead when all at once there was the hell of a noise – both bombs and ack-ack fire. We both dithered about, then threw ourselves onto the ground. We were smothered in dust, but there was no sign of a fire.

As soon as this little do was over we made for the shelter; however, my companion 'did not choose to stay in the middle of it', and so turned and fled in the opposite direction. After I reached the shelter there were one or two more silent dives followed by loud explosions.

Things then died down, and we could hear Hurricanes patrolling. Eventually, after about an hour, the Sergeant decided that there ought to be a sentry on the gate. We both went along and took up our positions together. We decided that if there should be another attack, we would take to the sandbagged pit, measuring about one yard square. There WAS another, about five minutes later. We both retired to the pit and made ourselves as small as possible. This time, Jerry came down almost right over us, and one bomb just about shook us to pieces, covering us with flying dust so that we could hardly breathe. Later we found that one bomb had landed about 20 yards away, and a land-mine only 10 yards from us. There were three dives, all much too close to us. The peculiar thing about all this was that I was not frightened. I could feel the Sergeant trembling where he touched me, but as far as I know, I was not shaking; in fact, I couldn't help laughing at ourselves in the middle of it. It was so comical to see the two of us cowering in such a small place.

At last, when things quietened down, we beat a hasty retreat to the shelter where we remained for the rest of the raid. It finished at about midnight. After it was all over, I went on guard again until 2.15. By then, I was pretty worm out. I had some bread and cheese then went to sleep for three hours. At 6 o'clock, when we were dismissed, I found a bit of shrapnel which had landed two feet from my head. The morning, at work, found me unresponsive, and I was given the rest of the day off. I felt a scrounger, but went to bed and slept the whole day. I guess that bomb shook me more than I thought; all the same, I did not mind being in the middle of it nearly as much as when I was alone by the Bofors. The worst part of the whole thing was the shrapnel; far more terrifying than the actual bombs.

I am sure that the sand took most of the force of the explosions. Had they been on solid ground the effects would have been far greater.

I suspect that I would have been nothing like as calm if the Sergeant had been more steady. Actually, he wasn't trembling, he was shaking. Reverse the roles, and I would have been in that state, not him. But there we are, that is commonplace; it is just a case of who lets go of his feelings first. As for the anonymous gentleman who scarpered, he should not have been allowed to get away with it. The sergeant should have hauled him back and sorted him out. His place of duty was the guard room, and he should have stayed there.

In spite of sleeping all day, I slept all night too! Somewhere else had the raid that night, and the following night it was in the Ismailia direction. However, Sunday the 7th made up for it. There were two raids, at 10 p.m. and 4 a.m, the first producing an enormous fire in the engine workshop, as we discovered in the morning.

I had a surprise that day: I ran into a fellow from school, MacKillop. He was a WO pilot on his way to Iraq. (Many years later, I learned that he was taken prisoner in Singapore, then lost his life when an allied submarine sank the Japanese prison ship in which he was being transported. I must have been one of the last Old Clayesmorians to talk to him.) It was good meeting him and being able to discuss familiar things in England, but it left me feeling guilty that I was not doing something more enterprising than maintaining aircraft. Fifty years on, and would I have made a pilot? No, I doubt if I would have qualified; my reactions were too slow, and even if I had, as a fighter pilot I would have been shot down at the first encounter which would have been a waste of one aeroplane. Bomber pilot perhaps: a certain amount of dogged determination might have come in useful, provided everything went according to plan – which it wouldn't have. The answer might have been navigator, but with my propensity for error, a flight to Berlin would probably have ended over Rome! So there we are – 'Whatever is, is best'.

The next night produced only one small raid, but that deposited a bomb outside the large hangar, and destroyed the watch office.

We suffered the last major attack on the night of Tuesday 9 August. We were out at dispersal when we heard it at 4 a.m. There was a huge fire and it looked like a mini London blitz. The disruption was such that our transport to bring us back to camp in the morning was very delayed and we did not finish breakfast until 10 a.m. It was on this occasion that I did my own version of 'If'. With lack of transport, everyone was flapping around at dispersal so I decided: 'If you can keep your head when all about you are losing theirs . . .' I sat down and wrote a letter, much to the annoyance of my companions – what an irritating fellow I must have been! – and I wonder why I had pen (before the days of Biros) and paper with me. But I see from my diary that, if in doubt, I was reading, or writing my diary or letters – and I am still doing it. You poor reader! During this particular raid one of the aircraft flying over us fired its guns. I, and others, did not like it.

Throughout the attacks Jerry had made a lot of use of delayed action

92

August 1941 – Abu Suier. Aftermath of the air raid on Tuesday 9th August 1941.

bombs. These had considerable nuisance value, and areas of Station were occupied by these nasty things. This last raid produced quite a crop of them; there was one in the Officers Mess which put that out of commission. To Erks' extreme annoyance the YMCA canteen was commandeered for the duration; however the stalwart Clifford, in charge of the canteen, declared that he would still tend our needs – at the back door presumably.

The Blenheim which we were working on had not been damaged, but we could not finish the job because of lack of tools. I suppose they had been destroyed in the raid.

Another crisis point was when we had to collect two propellers from a store where one of these bombs was sitting. We were joined in the task by Pilot Officer Donovan who lifted and heaved as much as anyone. He went up in our estimation no end, after having been the source of frequent criticism over the past few weeks.

By now, the Station was in a mess. It was still functioning, but far from efficiently. It had been a successful moon phase for the enemy. He had timed the raids for the full moon and, as I have already remarked, a full moon in Egypt is very bright; there are no clouds for it to hide behind. From the air, the whole camp must have been completely visible with all the key targets clearly identifiable. Workshops and stores had been destroyed and the whole maintenance programme disrupted.

Rumours were now to prove fact, and we were to move. On 17 September we said goodbye to Abu Suier.

Chapter 8

EGYPT FOR THE EGYPTIANS

Feluccas on the Nile   R.B.

It was time for these young eyes to look around and take in the surroundings; young eyes that were more familiar with the birds and the bees than shops, towns and people; which did not know England let alone foreign parts.

Unlike the modern school-boy, I did know a certain amount about Egypt from geography lessons. I knew of the Nile and the Battle thereof, of the Delta, of cotton crops, of the Pyramids and the Canal. I may not have known what they looked like, but when I left England's shores I had a vague idea of what to expect once I knew that Egypt was to be our destination. Egyptian faces, that was another matter; I suppose I assumed that they looked like Englishmen with darker complexions.

In past years, Egypt had outstripped Britain. A lot of men had used a lot of stones to build a lot of pyramids, while we in England had used fewer men, with fewer stones to build a much smaller Stonehenge.

15-love to Egypt. Then there was the Canal. Under Mr de Lesseps, the Egyptians had built a far bigger and deeper ditch than Offa had managed to achieve with his Dyke, which put the score up to 30-love. However, Disraeli had made a quick 'bob' out of it on the Stock Exchange, which evened things out again for the next hundred years until President Nasser and Anthony Eden got cross with one another. Mind you, I do wonder how the locals felt when the digging was in progress. They must have wondered whether removal of the last grain of sand from the ditch would result in an mighty torrent as the Mediterranean disgorged into the Red Sea.

The numbers game was still in operation in 1941 when I saw my first Egyptian train chugging into or out of Abu Suier station. The coaches were full, and descendants of those early builders were hanging on all over the outside, and sitting on the roofs of all the carriages. They were quite safe; there was no danger of heads being knocked off because there were no bridges for the train to go under, and the speed of travel was limited to about twenty miles per hour.

Although I had been in Egypt for over a month, I had seen practically nothing of it. A couple of drives along roads through miles of sand, and that was about it. Two or three brief afternoon excursions to Ismailia had displayed a mixture of East and West; there were emporia lining a shopping street but the shops were open at the front and were not organised with mahogany counters or smartly dressed young ladies at the tills. The purchase of an item was not a cut-and-dried affair; it required a lot of discussion about the merits of the article, and suggestions by both parties that it was worth either more or less than the sum named. There was no question of nipping into a shop to buy a pair of socks; the whole thing became a social event and took half the afternoon.

Many of the male populace one encountered in the street wore long-flowing, nightgown-like robes, each with a red fez perched on the top of dark-haired head. The ladies, rather less numerous than the men, were shrouded in black from head to toe.

There were some quite impressive buildings in the place, as well as a great deal of shanty town. The Canal Pilots building on the water front demanded a second look with its two storey imposing arcaded front, and three cupolas. There were a lot of good residential houses and a general air of prosperity.

The other impression was smell. Perhaps in England one was inured to local smells, but not so in Egypt, where the variety was enormous, ranging from oriental spices to straightforward nasty.

So far, my knowledge of Egypt was tiny, but now, on 17 September 1941 I was to venture further into this unknown country.

But oh dear, another queue; the RAF was forming up in line for its departure from Abu Suier, by lorry. Lots of them. I could not face it. A rough calculation told me that out of just over a year in the RAF, I had spent over three weeks standing in queues. Enough was enough. I would go later (I wonder why there was no roll-call?). I therefore returned to my billet and did my laundry. It had time to dry in the hot sun and I was ready to depart by a later lorry at 1 p.m.

I trust that my reader will not object too much to a short dissertation on queues; after all it was an important aspect of life in the ranks, and I feel justified in thinking that I had become an expert on the subject, and therefore qualified to hold forth for a paragraph or two.

The British are an orderly race, and expert at forming queues. This is greatly to our credit and far more civilised than the elbowing and frayed tempers one can encounter abroad. But, I ask, is the queuing not sometimes overdone?

Over the months, this thinking Erk evolved a queue philosophy which runs more or less as follows. There are three classes of queue:-
1. The obligatory queue which cannot be avoided.

2. Queues, which, if avoided, would cut off one's nose . . . etc.

3. Avoidable queues.

Examples of these might be:

1. Pay parade, parades ordered by higher authority for such things as collecting clothing from stores, or parades for medical injections. All very time consuming.

2. Lining up at the cookhouse because the smoked salmon might run out, missing the liberty bus to Cairo because the lorry was full, or being unable to get a seat at the ENSA concert because all were taken.

3. All other queues at which one loses nothing by biding one's time.

The majority of queues are completely voluntary and fall under the third category. It is only with experience that the novice discovers that he can put his time to much better use; having continued to play with his Meccano – or whatever – for an extra half hour, he can present himself at the desk, counter, table or alternative target, and get exactly what he wants without any trouble at all.

The herd instinct in human beings is an interesting phenomenon. Stand one hundred men at the corner of the parade ground, tell them that, shall we say, noodles are for sale over there, and with one accord, they will dash across to be first to be served. The fact that there are ample noodles to supply every man with all that he wants does not matter. Each man wants to be in front.

The same thing applies in civvy street. Take, for example, the 10.46 (or 10.79 o'clock under metric time!) from Folkestone to London. As we approach Charing Cross Station over the bridge, everyone gets up from his/her seat, elbows his/her neighbour when putting on his/her coat, then patiently waits in the gangway, cheek by jowl with the next him/her, until the train stops. Then, butting with suitcase or plastic bag, there is a general mêlée to the door, followed by another queue to pass through the ticket barrier. Meanwhile, Mr Experience remains seated, reading. As the last him/her departs the carriage he gets up, dons his coat, picks up his *Daily Telegraph* and walks calmly to the barrier, to emerge onto the concourse alongside the last him/her in the queue. He has saved himself much irritation, frustration and agitation, to no loss (unless he was running late for an appointment, in which case he should have been in number two category).

This was one of the great lessons I learned from my time in the ranks – much to the annoyance of my wife in later years, who declares that I am always the last to leave anywhere.

And so, my journey was far more comfortable in a lorry with fewer Erks, less kit and a greater opportunity to take in the route we travelled.

17 September 1941.

For the whole of the way to Cairo the road had the sweet water canal on the left and the railway on the right. I shouldn't think the height varied more than 10 – 20 feet along the whole of the 100 miles; there was just one slight up and down. It was a monotonous road, but interesting. We could see the water wheels being turned by blindfolded oxen, and the natives working in the 'fields'. We passed through a number of native villages which were the last word in squalor. The people were lying down among their donkeys and livestock, and everything swarmed with flies. There was no sanitation and the stink hit us as we drove along the road. The banks of the canal were lined with natives bathing, then next to them were others with flocks of sheep. Barges were sailing in the canal, loaded with bricks and all sorts of commodities.

From time to time we passed an upturned lorry where it had gone down the bank, off the road. We passed dozens of natives on their tiny donkeys, and it was funny to see their arms and legs all flapping and the whole outfit looking thoroughly top heavy. It was funny, too, to see the loads of crops walking along the road – or so it appeared until one got closer and saw a camel underneath; one beast we passed must have been loaded at least 10 feet wide.

Sweet water. My geography lessons had told me nothing about that, but enquiry spelt out the answer in words of one syllable – if salt water was bitter, then fresh water was sweet. *QED*.

Fresh water, the all-important life giver. One only had to look around to see mile after mile after mile of sand where the water was not. This canal drew a pattern across the desert, a green swathe varying in width from a mile to fifty yards; a veritable artery on which the whole of life, animals, crops and humans, depended. Thus one witnessed within a small confine every aspect of human existence. This water was used for all purposes. I like to think that a pipe produced fresh water for drinking, but this was unlikely – and thereby hangs a tale! The Egyptians, who consumed this fluid, appeared to suffer no ill effects; but suppose one of us had lapped a few mouthfuls. I suspect that we would have been struck down and probably ended in the mortuary. We are talking about the natural resistance of the human body to bacteria. Speaking personally, I am firmly convinced that the modern fetish for hygiene is doing us no good. The human body acts with strength to privation, so is the converse not true? The more we pamper and disinfect, the more flabby we become. Our bodies no longer have resistance to these ills, so that we fall victim to every unwashed can. I even go so far as to say that one should make a deliberate point of allowing contamination of everyday things to help one's body fight disease. From my soap box, I extend my theory to include excessive central heating with the consequent glut of the common cold. I become dangerous on my soap box so I had better stop. I only ask for a little common-sense in all things.

The canal acted as a public well, (I am writing of 1941, not 1995),

100

washing place and receptacle for every kind of rubbish. The Nile was this life giver. When the water had started on its journey 3,500 miles away, it was clean and pure, but on its way to the sea, it had become the depository for more and more foreign matter. No doubt, as long as it was a mighty river, it was quite able to cope with these additional ingredients, but once it reached the intensely populated Delta, it was fighting a losing battle. This particular canal, the same as every other canal in Egypt, was being fed by the waters of the Nile, and though masquerading under the title of 'canal', because it was man-made, water was being taken in at one end from the river and discharged out at the other into the sea. I never tested the truth of this, but there was a flow from west to east running parallel with the Cairo-Ismailia road.

The harnessing of the Nile had taken place in the nineteenth century when the main canals were built; however, because the system did not work very efficiently, the good old British were called in. They rebuilt the Barrage in 1883 so that the all-important silt poured into the canals instead of being filtered out. This ensured the continued fertility of the Delta dating back to pre-history, but only upset when man intervened.

The volume of water in the Nile varied enormously throughout the seasons because it was governed by the rainfall thousands of miles away in the highlands of Abyssinia and East Africa. It was a complex business to control this flow, but a series of barrages, dams and sluices did the job. The water which we now saw as we drove along the road in our lorry was probably the freshest for any time in the year, because the flow of the Nile reached its zenith in October.

The most noble sights on the Nile and canals were the feluccas, the native craft. With their triangular sails suspended from the huge sloping boom fastened at the bow and reaching upwards to a height almost twice the length of the vessel, they dipped majestically in time to the gentle flow of the water, unhurried and stately in their progress. The cargos could be absolutely anything: livestock, cotton, modern merchandise. On more than one occasion I saw a lorry or car on the deck. I am told that because of the prevailing wind from the north, these vessels were able to sail up the Nile against the strong flow; their sails certainly had a large catchment area. As we passed, it was incongruous to see His Egyptian Majesty's modern motor-yacht anchored in the canal near his private domain. Needless to say, his private house was set in a beautifully wooded area – a haven of peace and luxury amid the squalor.

The canal provided water for the 'fields' – what resemblance to fields in Dorset? – standing quite a few feet above canal water level, so modern technology had to be used to lift this water to a higher plain! Oxen. Oxen walking round in circles yoked to a contraption which, through devious mechanical means ultimately filled little buckets which spewed water into a channel. A network of small ditches and dykes then allowed the whole area to be irrigated. A maxi Romney Marsh! As for the crops, I have memories of tall growing plants which must have been sweetcorn, and on a lower level, rice and cotton. Where ploughing was in progress, it was the sort of scene depicted in prints of medieval Britain.

The people we saw all along the road and in their villages were the fellahin, the poorest class in the land. Men and animals lived together at a more or less identical standard of living; the women wearing their black clothes sat outside their little flat roofed huts grinding grain in their mortars. Oh what a contrast to our orderly life in England where, indeed, there was poverty, but on nothing like the scale I was now seeing.

At last, we sighted Cairo. The desert appeared to extend to the very outskirts of the city, a city combining the very modern with relics of antiquity. The main streets are wide boulevards, with one way traffic down each side of grass islands. The buildings are six to eight storeys high, very modern with hotels, cinemas and office blocks; but in the middle of all this, traffic is held up for a train crossing the main road. Taxis are horse drawn carriages, and at one point we almost removed the nose of a horse pulling a hearse with funeral procession following. Away from the centre, the native streets are shanty town. We crossed the Nile, which looked filthy, but the view from the bridge was worth seeing.

During the course of the next nine months I made many visits to Cairo. My first Liberty to Cairo was on 22 August and I formed this initial impression.

Cairo, Midan Emad-el-Dine. Cars and garrys.

103

During the afternoon it was surprising how deserted everywhere was, and yet it all came to life after dark. Without the partial blackout the city must be very impressive – much more so than in daylight.

There are a few points I do not like, the chief being the obnoxious smells which hang in the air. Also the number of street beggars; one cannot progress 10 yards without some vendor thrusting razor blades, shoe laces or other commodity in one's face, not to mention shoe-shine boys. They don't take no for an answer and the only thing to do is to ignore them.

With time, one grew to like it, and the smells merged to become Cairo. We were told that many of the babies carried by beggars were not their own; it was a begging industry. There was also a lot of street entertainment – organ grinders, jugglers, acrobats and all the fun of the fair. There was always something to look at.

It was a cosmopolitan city where East meets West, a gateway to the hinterland of Africa, and to the rest of the Middle East, swollen to capacity by the war. There were refugees from southern Europe and troops adding to the number of peace-time residents. As one walked down the streets every language bombarded one's ears, and from memory I would say that the French and Greek tongues predominated.

It was a land of extreme wealth and poverty; the rabbit warrens of the poor shanty town stretched for miles, but along the banks of the Nile and on Gezira Island there were avenues of modern luxury houses and flats. Further out in the suburbs, Helwan, Maardi and Heliopolis compared favourably with the spas of western Europe. Heliopolis in particular had a fine colonnaded main street, and some private buildings that needed to be seen to be believed; one of them, The Baron's Folly was a mixture of the Baroque and Hinduism, a pink stone edifice covered with carvings, and so ornate that it was like an iced cake.

I was lucky to have access to a more luxurious life than my fellow Erks; my stepbrother John was a Major on the staff of GHQ, and he had a flat on Gazira Island, complete with roof garden and servant. I could go there any time, enjoy a hot bath, sit down to a good meal and generally escape the less congenial side of life. One or two of his friends had cars, so that from time to time I could be whisked around to see the sights under self-propulsion. I was taken to the Zoo, with its imposing columned entrance and basse relief tableau to each side. However, I was more interested to see the English flowers in bloom than the rather mangy animals behind bars.

The heart of Cairo is the Citadel. Standing on its rocky hill it dominates the city, with the avenue Mohammed Ali leading almost to it. As one crossed the Nile by the main bridge, the imposing Kasr-el-Nil barracks reminded one of similar establishments in the UK.

The name Shepheards Hotel is almost as well known as Cairo itself. I was fortunate enough to step inside and have tea on the famous terrace, complete with Palm Court Orchestra playing. There was nothing wrong with Groppe's either, where the most luscious cakes tempted themselves off the display stands. Of a more intellectual nature, there were museums with their collections of unrivalled Egyptian antiquity (One visit only!).

Something more up my street was the Opera House, opened in November 1869 in the same month as the Suez Canal. Verdi was commissioned by the Khedive of Egypt, Ismail Pasha, to write an opera. Verdi delved into Egyptian history, and the result was *Aida* which had its premiere at the Opera House on 24 December 1871. Not quite in the same vein, I attended a performance of *The Gondoliers* and would willingly have paid more visits had the opportunity arisen. It was a fine building, but constructed mainly of wood, and subsequently burned down. What a pity.

Rue Suliman Pasha and other main boulevards were on a par with western cities. The Immobilia Building at 14 storeys in Rue Kasr-el-Nil would not have shamed London and the view down onto the Medan Amed-el-Din – where motor traffic and horse-drawn fiacres alternated – could have stepped out of the 1920s in any European city. (My photograph shows horsedrawn garrys and motor vehicles side by side.) But get away from the Western Quarter and one was back into squalor and poverty with the sound of Arab music pouring out of every hovel plus a gargantuan mixture of smells. The Muski (an equivalent of the Paris Flea Market, I suppose) offered every commodity under the sun and where nothing changed hands until after at least half an hour's haggle. Following such an experience one stopped for a tiny cup of Turkish or other coffee sitting outside the emporium.

Being such a cosmopolitan city, many religions were represented; there were churches of every branch of the Christian faith ranging from Roman Catholic through Syrian, Armenian to Coptic, and of course, the Muslim mosques where the sound of the mullars calling the host to prayer at regular intervals echoed across the city.

For an Erk, the gravitation points in the city were the canteens, and they served us well. Apart from the usual things that rankers do, our main entertainment was the cinema. There were dozens of them and with the number of films in circulation there was always something to see. They were out-door establishments, so one sat out under the stars with the noises of the city acting as a background to the most tender love scenes.

Cairo. A city where every need could be met one hundredfold, where shortages and rationing could be forgotten, where gluttony in every conceivable form could be indulged. Whatever the shortcomings of food in our own cook house, the balance could be corrected on Liberty day.

This was far from our bombed and rationed homeland; and we did not spare ourselves.

Chapter 9

KM 17

Kilometre 17 on the El Faiyum road to the south of Cairo. Shades of Three Men in a Boat, but this time it was sand. Having spent the night in a large marquee on some very hard ground, I had to team up with anyone who was willing, find a tent, then erect it. As total beginners at this art we were in a bit of a muddle, and of course the wind got up at the vital moment so that canvas billowed in all directions. The first attempt was a failure, but second time round we achieved our purpose in one and a half hours. We found a hurricane lamp, and after dark, with the flap down, it was quite cosy.

19 August 1941.
We all woke up with the firm intention of not going to work, but before long we changed our minds, either because we were ordered to do so, or conscience – the latter in my case. Being Friday it was

pay-day which took two solid hours, leaving very little time for work.

Someone acquired a water can lid to act as a basin, civilisation was coming to Km 17.

On the Sunday we had our first Liberty to Cairo. The RAF provided a bus (i.e. lorry) to Mena, then it was a matter of a lift in anything that moved, or by tram. In fact, one nearly always found a lift; there was military traffic all the time and quite often there was a spare seat in a staff car. Although water was not rationed in camp, it was all brought by bowzer and in limited supply. (On 27 December we ran out of water completely – no washing!). First call in Cairo was nearly always the YMCA for a shower, followed by shop gazing. I bought my first camera.

22 August 1941.
Out of bed at 5.40, then a half hour wait for breakfast.

You will understand my earlier remarks about queuing. Self-help produced a bedside locker and I found some straw for filling my palliasse – greater luxury at night!

Probably the most important thing from the morale point of view was post. We were greedy for letters but they took so long. It was about this time that air graphs were introduced. An air graph form was a single sheet of paper about foolscap size; there was an address space at the top and the rest of the page was available for the 'letter'. The completed page was photographed on 35 mm, and the film was flown home. At the other end, a print about a quarter the size of the original was delivered by ordinary post. Transmission time was only a few days, so we felt we were in closer touch with home. There was a reciprocal service from UK to overseas.

Work on aircraft was nearly all on Blenheims; perhaps I had just gravitated to them, but it certainly helped to know one's way around a type of aircraft. I found myself doing inspections as well as specific repairs. Quite soon after arriving at Km 17 we found a fault in a brake drum, due no doubt to sand on the pad. We had to send back to Abu Suier for a replacement but, by the time it arrived, similar faults had been found in other aircraft, and we lost our spare to a higher priority machine. There were times when a balance had to be struck between Peter and Paul.

A little light relief was provided when I was given a job on a Tomahawk, and on 9 March a Free French fighter needed a wheel change.

I was still not very professional at my job, and I have a note of spending most of one afternoon battling with a split-pin which I could not remove. I feel sure that a bit of know-how could have saved a lot of time and energy. In March I had some splicing to do, and on another occasion a couple of us managed to damage a tail wheel through ham fistedness. One had to learn, but at least this error was not serious enough to endanger the aircraft in flight.

15 October 1941.

At 4.45 I went up in a Blenheim for the first time. Looking out of the window one saw just space with the Nile and the Pyramids far below – and sand. Our camp looked like a model, just a few dots for tents, dark patches for aircraft, and a dark ribbon of road. The roof was open and it was very chilly. When we were above the clouds I went to the turret. A lovely sight, like a carpet of silver down with the sun glistening on the crests of the billows as it sank out of sight.

At the end of a servicing, members of the ground crew were allowed to have a flip in the aircraft when it went up for test flight – quite a good way of ensuring that they did the job properly!

109

For one reason or another, I calculate that I spent at least fifty per cent of my time not working. I have continual references in my diary such as:

12 October 1941.
I don't know why it is but when I get near a machine there automatically seems to be nothing to do.

21 October 1941. (and again on 23 October)
I've spent quite a large portion of the afternoon reading in the cockpit. It was draughty outside.

26 October 1941.
There hasn't been any work. I have quite publicly been making myself a knee table with no comment from the Flight Sergeant.

10 November 1941.
Still no work to do; there appears to be a deficiency of Blenheims.

And so it went on, through December and for as long as I was with 108 MU. While I did not normally go around agitating for work, I was very critical of this idleness. Sometimes I did do a bit of badgering, such as on 27 and 28 January; the result on this occasion was that I was given the task of changing a window in a Blenheim. A fiddly job which I found quite difficult.

As well as our tradesmen duties we were inevitably called upon to help with the general administration of the camp. Guard duties were not very arduous and gave one extra time off during the working day; a plus mark. And then there were cook-house duties lasting a week, forty-eight hours on duty, then twenty-four hours off; another plus mark and one could scoff extra rations. I was bounced into my first on 30 September and one of my tasks was to get up at 4 a.m. to light the field boilers. These cast-iron contraptions had a fire box below and a caldron above.

5 October 1941.
In the early hours of this morning one airman nearly met his end. To encourage burning, he threw paraffin into the fire box, and flames blew back into his face.

Damage was not too serious but it taught him not to be a bloody fool. A second session of cook house duties at the end of November put me in a quandary. I was put in charge of THE BREAD. No, don't laugh, it was a serious matter! With an assistant I had to cut it into slices and lob it out. With my orderly mind I insisted on doing the lobbing, and here I encountered a problem. The ration was two slices per man, but if there were any slices left over after everyone had filed through, then the spare was available on a 'first come, first served' basis. I stuck to this system strictly, but of course my 'friends' wanted a third piece at the outset. I was not going to indulge in favouritism, and I stuck to my guns, making myself unpopular in the process. One morning, my assistant did not materialise and there were insufficient slices cut by breakfast time. The rabble took over, and I got very angry. I was NOT going to have my bread hacked into chunks with insufficient for the men at the back of the queue. I needed a stripe on my arm (NCO I/C Bread!).

Meanwhile, on 7 December the Japanese attacked Pearl Harbour, and my sojourn in the cook-house looked even more depressing.

The food was not good. Even to this day I never want to meet bully beef or tinned pilchards again. I used to buy jam in Cairo, and as often as not, bread and jam was my evening meal. After some time I acquired a small stove and we used to give ourselves a brew-up in the tent. We became quite good at toast and eggs – on those occasions when we managed to get the eggs.

For Christmas day in 1941, the cook-house put on a feast as good as Mum would have prepared. With the ignorance of big-headed youth, some of us (and I admit that I had my tick too) found reason to grumble. If we can have a meal like this at Christmas, why is the food so terrible for the rest of the time? The fact that they had pulled out all the stops, and spent a lot of RAF Unit funds for this very special occasion escaped us. We were lucky to get this feast, rather than being unlucky not to have it for the rest of the time; but some will always grizzle.

We were accommodated six men to a 180 pounder tent. This allowed room for the palliasses plus sufficient space for one's kit. In the course of time I made myself a locker and a book shelf (plus the aforementioned knee table), and eventually luxury of luxuries – a piece of carpet. I have never believed in being uncomfortable if a little self-help can provide the answer. I have a confession to make, too. Brother John gave me his spare camp bed plus a fleecy quilt. I wonder why my companions didn't rib me unmercifully.

At the outset, our tent was just planted on top of the sand, but with experience we learned some desert law. Better to dig in. In due course we set to with shovels and dug a hole more than a foot deep, then erected the tent over this hole. This made it far more wind and dust-proof which was something we needed at this time of the year. A sandbag wind-break at the entrance, and low wall all the way round completed the defences.

It came as a great surprise to me that it could be so cold in the desert; on the morning of 6 January 1942, the sand was white with frost when we emerged from the tent. Even daytime could be uncomfortably cold when there was no sun, or the wind was blowing, to such an extent that on more than one occasion I wore my UK blue uniform to Cairo – and on 3 January, I used my greatcoat. As for the dust storms, they were difficult to bear.

16 January 1942.
My first real sand-storm. I can hardly breathe and everything is covered with dust. It started just before lunch and I lost my way coming back to the tent. I was unable to see more than 10 feet ahead. It was impossible to work in the afternoon.

These storms happened fairly frequently during the winter months, and they left everything, including oneself, covered with fine sand. A bath was the only answer, but that had to wait until the next visit to the YMCA in Cairo.

On 15 December we had rain, the first I had seen in Egypt and very refreshing too after the hot spell we had recently been having.

Another interesting manifestation was on 9 March when we had an invasion of ladybirds; thousands of them swarming over everything, into the water, you name it. Migrating I suppose, but a lot of them could not have arrived at where they were going.

Apart from working on aeroplanes and hanging about reading, how did we spend our time? We had a NAAFI in camp but that was not geared to festivities. I should say that the most consistently popular outlet was to Mena where there was a cinema. Being only 17 kms away, we could usually get a lift both ways and pop into the canteen down there for a char and wad before coming back to camp.

Liberty to Cairo was, theoretically, once per week but from time to time this was stopped for one reason or another. On the other hand it could be more frequent such as when on cook-house duties (the forty-eight hours on, twenty-four hours off system), so that an extra trip could be fitted in. We could apply for overnight passes; these allowed us to depart camp after end of work prior to a day off, and spend the night away. This suited me well. I applied as often as I could and spent the night at Brother John's flat at Zamalek. Others were not so fortunate. I revelled in the civilised surroundings; hot bath, proper breakfast and food, and company I was used to.

Apart from that, my main occupation was reading. My nose was permanently in a book, or I was writing letters. I have remarked that mail was all-important, and I am astonished at the number of letters I received. All sorts of unlikely people wrote to me, and I would reply by return of post. They must have got completely fed up with my non-stop writing.

The air-raids did not follow us from Abu Suier, but even so we had a couple of warnings during November, sufficient to ensure that all hurricane lamps were doused, leaving us sitting in darkness in the desert. There was the usual scuttle in all directions while I stayed put.

The camp was more or less self-contained with its own medical section and small sick bay. I found myself in the latter for a few days with sandfly fever. This was a sort of mini malaria, and I ran a high temperature for a couple of days, but recovery was quick, and I lived to tell the tale.

I cannot allow our in-camp entertainment to pass unnoticed. I refer to the 'Bodgers', otherwise known as the 'Seven Singing Sisters'. They were the road makers. We were inhabiting a bit of virgin desert so that it had to be made into an RAF camp with roads. The apparatus for this was in the hands of the Egyptians who duly arrived with a tar mixing machine and lots of bodies. They set up their witches coven and went to work, heating the tar and pouring it onto the sand. (There must have been more to it than that, but the detail escapes me). They had no steam-roller and this was where the Bodgers came in. A gang of them – more than seven in fact – lined up across the strip of newly laid tarmac armed with plungers. They then advanced slowly to the rhythmic measure of their leaders chant. Ya yu yum – bonk; ya yu yum – bonk; and so this happy noise went on by the hour as they progressed steadily round the camp, leaving a tarmac road behind them. I took some photographs of them which they greatly appreciated, grinning their heads off.

114

The British sense of humour is never far away, and we enjoyed our Bodgers. Humour also led to us making the most of things like the crane episode. I don't suppose it was really very funny, but it gave us something to laugh at.

12 November 1941.
We went to fetch a couple of cranes on a lorry, and with Flight-Sergeant K in charge it was a bit chaotic. We nearly upset one crane from the trailer *en route*, only saving it by a determined effort; then we got stuck in the sand so that we had to be towed out. Finally in the unloading we managed to upset the other one. Pickfords would have managed better.

Most people have a sense of humour tucked away somewhere. We had a Flight-Sergeant who would bark at us, but we came to realise that when he barked he had a twinkle in his eye. If we wanted something from him, we would invariably be greeted with a refusal, but then after a bit of 'argy bargy', as often as not, he would relent, and we would get what we wanted. It all depended upon attitude.

Attitude is all important, and I learned this lesson for myself. I wanted to apply for a pass, but was late doing so. Another fellow had already applied but had been refused; however, I thought I would have a go. I duly went to see 'authority' and was told, 'No. You are too late.' I stood my ground, did a bit of explaining, plus a bit of reasoning, and the result was that both my own pass and the other fellow's was accepted. Following this episode, I remarked:

Thinking about the pass yesterday, I'm beginning to realise that the only way to get things done is to put oneself in the foreground. If I hadn't argued yesterday, I would have been refused my pass.

I was learning something which should have dawned ages before. Moving to a teaching context, this was probably one of my earliest lessons in how to put a subject across. The seeds of a teaching career had been sown as a result of all my reading of history, and in the following chapter you will discover how my mind was working. Here for the first time, as an adult, I had registered how a positive attitude could influence the outcome of a situation.

Returning to humour, there was plenty to laugh about in the following episode, but it also had a rather more serious side to it.

12 February 1942.

It all started yesterday when a notice was sent round saying that, in future, we should shave and be fully dressed for parade. I fully support this.

14 pegs, with numbers on them, were driven into the 'parade ground', where we usually muster. That was alright, but during the night somebody removed them and put them outside the CO's office. Liberty was immediately cancelled; we were given a lecture, told that the culprit should own up, and also told that if any further attempt was made on the 'crown pegs', a 12-man picket would be detailed to guard them. This put everybody in a bolshie mood.

During the afternoon a plot was hatched up to remove the pegs once and for all during the night. Half the camp appeared to be in favour of this, but I declined to join in. I can see both points of view, but it seems to me as being hopeless to continue fighting a war if we can't have union in our own camp. I think the officers are right. There are faults on both sides, but the men in the ranks won't take a single order, they always grizzle at anything we are told to do. The argument appears to be that we are fighting for freedom, therefore

116

officers should not be our superiors. That may be all right for peace time, but in war, men must do what they are told without question. If they don't, what's the result? Chaos. We have a stubborn crowd in the ranks who are fighting against their own country.

13 February 1942.
The comedy has continued in grand style. As arranged, the pegs were removed during the night, but by a lesser number of people than expected. There was no reaction from the 'Powers That Be' except that Corporal Kay was detailed for night peg guard – but this was subsequently cancelled. Meanwhile, a new set of pegs being made in the carpenter's shop were removed at lunch time. I did not witness the pantomime that followed the discovery, but marvellous stories went around – many officers arrived at the scene to act as detectives. The Special Police were called in; they looked for missing pegs everywhere, even with magnifying glasses so the story went! All very funny, but imagine our surprise when, leaving work, more pegs were in position. They are supposed to be painted with wet paint so as to identify any criminal who takes them overnight.

14 February 1942.
They've disappeared again. No drastic results yet, and no one covered with paint. During the day, another set has been placed in position, but I understand that they will not be taken tonight because of the 'Tomahawk Ball' next Saturday. Rumour says that Liberty will be cancelled for three months.

15 February 1942.
The pegs stayed in position, but discipline in general is being

117

tightened up. We are told that anyone late for parade will be put on a charge, and that the dining hall will be out of bounds between 7 a.m. and 6.30 p.m.

Loss of the dining hall was a nasty blow. It was a refuge in a 'building' where one could write letters at a table. Mind you, to do so during the working day was scrounging.

15 February 1942.
Someone tried to remove the pegs last night but was caught. What a bloody fool, acting on his own. It was obvious the Special Police were on the look out. Liberty has been restored. The remaining peg-pullers have not even suggested owning up, which I think is pretty bad. A difficult thing to do, but at least they should have considered doing so instead of leaving one man to take all the blame.

This whole episode sheds a light on the feelings running through the Erk strata at this particular RAF station at the time. (It would be dangerous to generalise, and I did not compare notes with men at other stations). We had been allowed to come and go as we pleased far too freely. My diary makes constant reference to not going to work on time, and we were getting away with it. When discipline is allowed to slip to such an extent, then it is difficult to reimpose it. There was the occasional parade but one wonders why we did not have a muster parade each morning at a specified time, where the roll would have been called, and we would have been marched off to work. Had this been done from the time that we arrived at KM 17 the tone for the working day would have been set, and discipline easily enforced. When it comes to the point, I suppose all stops had been pulled out to get the technical side of the Unit operating and man management had taken second priority.

I supported the officers in this fracas, and it was thoughts such as this which led to my metamorphosis.

Chapter 10

METAMORPHOSIS

I had been in the RAF for nearly eighteen months so it was time to take stock. I was that much older and so, theoretically, more sensible, and I had the guiding influence of Brother John. He was doing his best for me.

Was I content? The answer was no; I was neither fish nor fowl. I was not achieving satisfaction from my job as an aircraft rigger, and companionship of the sort I understood, was missing. A man, however, immature, must enjoy one of those two ingredients if life is to be worthwhile.

What was wrong with the rigging? My following comments are not complimentary towards the RAF, so when reading them you should remember my negative approach to the whole thing when I joined up. I have no doubt that a more thrusting and self-possessed animal would have done better; however, that was not possible in my case, and I still think that, handled differently, I could have made a good tradesman, leading to further advancement in the Blue.

Before exploring any further, we need to look at my favourite subject: teaching. At Halton we had been taught a great deal of both theory and skills. The teaching was excellent and we came away from there after six months with a good basic knowledge of what we were required to do to aeroplanes, but, it was nearly all bench knowledge. For example, we had seen the hydraulics of a real aeroplane, BUT that represented only a very small percentage of our learning time. I am sure that most people will agree that 'I like to be shown how to do it on the real thing'. There are so many little dodges and practical know-hows. The know-how can make the difference of ten minutes and save frustration, even with something like taking a screw out of an inaccessible place. In other words, the knowledge picked up on a formal course does not finish the job; a period of apprenticeship is required to round off the learner and to turn him into a craftsman.

It follows from the above argument that our Halton trained rigger still had a lot to learn, and the only person he could learn it from was an already skilled and experienced rigger. The solution should have been to place him with such a person in a crew for a couple of months or more. The Corporal in charge would then have been able to check on the 'trainee's' work and tell him how to go about the job in a business-like manner – such as the split-pin episode. At the end of those two months the Halton trained rigger would have had the knowledge and confidence to work on his own, and confidence plays a very large part – except to the big headed! This did not happen to your author who was almost totally devoid of confidence, and thus never overcame the first hurdle of being sure that he had put the two pieces together satisfactorily. And if there is one thing that destroys the recognition by a superior of a man's ability, it is prolonged dithering when approaching a task. In other words, I was not fit to be put on a job to do it myself.

From Blue to Khaki

Such was the theory, but what happened in practice? With a break of four months between finishing at Halton and next doing any work on an aeroplane, I was put alongside an engine fitter – not my trade, and thereafter, I never seemed to get settled. Of course, at Abu Suier, everything was in turmoil because of the enemy bombing, but I reckon that the officers in charge of the squadron were not extracting maximum potential from their manpower. On arrival at the new location at Km 17 we lacked spares for a time which left us idle, but again I was not put with a crew. My diary makes constant reference to 'doing nothing', or sitting in a cockpit reading. I was not scrounging or malingering; I was simply not given the work, and so it became a vicious circle. Time dragged on, and I note that one senior NCO told me that I was useless at my job. I need not have been.

Against this deficiency, I possessed a quality which was eventually recognised by Sergeant Dowell. I could organise things quite well, and did not like a muddle. I am not sure how he spotted this, but I was put in charge of the squadron stores which held not only small items required as regular replacements (Blenheim tyres for instance), but also specialised tools, booked out for a particular job then returned to store.

When all is said and done, this situation did not auger well for a war-time career in the RAF.

The second problem: relationships with my companions. This is the difficult part, to be honest but not biased; not to be superior or condescending, but to recognise fairly the merits of both points of view.

I found myself living in a tent with five other men, two Australian and three British. I would not say they were the rough sort, but on the other hand they were not concerned in the more academic subjects that I found interesting. I was forever reading history; that present from my aunt which I mentioned earlier, H.A.L. Fisher's *History of Europe* arrived on 17 February 1942, and I was content to sit down and read it. Likewise I read

122

Bryant's *Charles II*, a biography of Cecil Rhodes, and a volume of Goldsmith which I bought in Cairo. Needless to say, I could not discuss these subjects with anyone after I had done my reading, so it was a solitary occupation and I was out on a limb. Conversely, things which interested the other five were of no concern to me. There were long arguments and discussions about communism and socialism and I joined in, but my views did not necessarily coincide with theirs; on balance I think I agreed with them, but I had reservations and would sometimes make it plain that I thought differently. I was also trailing them by quite a long way in experience and maturity.

K.M. 17. Tent companions, Fisher, Kinnoch, Hyder, Morton, Howard

123

One way and another I am surprised that they put up with me as willingly as they did. I was a naïve public school prat, and they could have made life pretty unbearable had they wished. On the contrary, they did what they could to help me, and I remember one particular incident which shows how thoughtful they could be. I had picked up a word which rolled off the tongue rather nicely, and I introduced it into my conversation not infrequently; eventually one of my tent companions, Morton, asked me quietly if I knew what it meant. No. So he told me, and I never used it again. I had lived with my head in the sand, but in fairness, there were so many aspects of their life which were totally foreign to me, mainly because of a difference in background. Extremely good for me, but that did not alter the fact that I felt like a fish out of water.

There was another problem, too, which might be summed up as initiative. My diary makes frequent references to everybody grumbling and doing nothing to help themselves. There was a sandstorm blowing and it was coming into the tent at the end where the flap was open. Did anybody do anything about it? No. I was the one who had to close the flap at that end and open the one at the other end where the sand was not coming in. There was an awful lot of talk but very little of the 'help yourself'. I, on the other hand, had been brought up with the help yourself doctrine to the fore. I must confess that this side of life exasperated me, and it kept on happening. My strict upbringing had ensured that I did a good job and used my head. Perhaps it was all part of the difference between two types of education: mine at a public school designed to produce leadership, and the others at run-of-the-mill establishments concerned mainly with just the three Rs. Anyway, whatever the reason, I became aware that a fundamental difference in approach existed between my companions and myself.

Fifteen months in the RAF, and I was little more than a floating mess, bound to my role by neither technical skill nor real compatibility with my companions. I had discovered how easy it is to lose one's individuality in a crowd. Imperceptively, one's standards change and one takes on a new identity. I found this was happening to me. Perhaps it is insulting to my fellows, but nevertheless true, to suggest that without a good kick up the backside, my descent into oblivion would find me ending the war still as an Erk. Shame on me. Was this the best I could do?

Fortunately, there was a third factor in the equation: Brother John.

Meeting John had an immediate effect upon my whole attitude. I met him for the first time on 1 October. Only one week later on 7 October, on my next Liberty to Cairo, I had sorted myself out to such an extent that I bought some better clothing. I had also resolved that I would not haunt the lowest, cheapest and scruffiest of canteens for my casual cups of tea. An unseen hand had grabbed me by the scruff of the neck and started to pull me into shape.

Within a few weeks, I had taken a further step towards self-betterment. John had persuaded me to take French lessons. There was a large French contingent in Cairo, and it was not difficult to find a coach. I visited her once a week, or as often as I could manage, and found myself trying to write French essays back at camp. Do you wonder that I was not quite in tune with my tent companions? I was starting to look into the future and, for the first time, work out what I was going to do after the war. It was time to stop free-wheeling. I began to think about a BA to qualify me for teaching, especially history, geography and english. I sought the opinion of my ex house master JDS. He agreed, but said I would never live to be rich. In the shorter term, John raised the subject of a commission in the Army. My reaction, without much thought was: 'Why not. I think I am no worse than what I can see of the RAF officers.' Not exactly a ball of fire, but better than nothing. What a bit of cheek!

Last but not least, John shared a flat on Ghezerah island with a Major and a Lieutenant-Colonel (both subsequently killed in the Western Desert).

125

I was relaxed in their company, and the surroundings compared with home. I was made aware of what I was missing.

Responsibility, command – call it what you will. I have mentioned occasions when I considered – at the time – that discipline in the RAF went adrift: the riot on the *Eastern Prince* at Aden; the pegs at Km 17; the man who ran away when on guard at Abu Suier. I am not saying that all these incidents were typical, but on the two former occasions I disagreed with the men and sided with the officers, and I have said my piece about the latter.

The peg incident introduces another point, too. One man was eventually caught. He was a fool to operate on his own. He was only one of many involved but he took the can for the lot. I did not approve at the time, and I ask myself whether I would have come forward and acknowledged participation under the circumstances. I don't know, but I do know that if I had not, then conscience would still be with me. Conscience is an awkward thing and has a habit of nagging. I quote one small example which I have never got rid of. Returning from the Far East on SS *Strathnaven* in 1948, sharing my cabin with five other officers, I had a large box of gramophone records which occupied a begrudged space on the floor. I had, as did we all, a highly valued bottle of gin at a time when this commodity was worth its weight in gold in the UK. In the cabin one day, a bottle of gin, standing on the floor by me (goodness knows why it was there) broke. Gin flowed across the floor and I was accused of kicking it. I declared vigorously that I had not done so, and did not relent. With hindsight, I must have been responsible even though I was not aware of it. I never apologised, or offered my own bottle to the loser. Justice had out, though. In the course of time I discovered that the gin had seeped into the record box and that the shellac surface had been eaten off quite a number of the records. Every time I played one of the damaged records I was reminded of my sin. Oh conscience. I could mention far worse conscience prickers, but will not!

All this is completely incidental to the situation I found myself in, but it does give some indication of my mental approach to responsibility.

I am in the unusual position of being able to compare man management and leadership between the Army and the RAF, having served in both at the receiving end. I have an extremely clear memory, not recorded in my diary, of an incident I experienced shortly after my transfer to the Royal Armoured Corps. I went to the orderly room one evening after normal working hours and found a young subaltern sitting on the corner of a table chatting informally to two or three Troopers. I stopped in my tracks and gawped. Never, not once in the whole of my time in the RAF, had I seen such a thing. Perhaps I had always been in the wrong place at the wrong time, but the fact remains that such close contact between officers and men was unknown to me.

From my experience, there was an entirely different relationship between officers and men in the two services, and I therefore pause to ask why.

My answer is that the two services engage in entirely different types of military operations. An RAF aircrew is not leading men; it is fighting its own battle far up in the sky. Compare this with the section, platoon and company commanders in the Army who are actually with their men, setting an example and leading them into battle.

One can delve deeper: the mental approach of men in the two services. In the RAF, the efficiency and success of the service depends to a very great extent on technical achievement, not only in the actual creation of the aircraft itself, but the handling of such complex technical equipment by most highly skilled crew in the air, and by the ground staff on the airfield. It is not surprising therefore that the outlook of the RAF man is ninety per cent technical to only ten per cent sheer leadership. Generally speaking, RAF officers are primarily technicians and boffins, more concerned with machines than men.

The army is the reverse. There is plenty of highly sophisticated and technical equipment in every regiment and corps of the Army, but ultimately every man is a soldier, and in the last resort is dependent upon 'teammanship' with his fellows in section, platoon, radio section or whatever. It is not therefore surprising that far greater importance is placed on leadership in the Army, and leadership in turn depends upon close familiarity of the officer with the men under his command. This can only be achieved through constant and regular personal contact.

To put it in a nutshell, to the RAF the machine is of overriding importance, whereas in the Army it is the Man. I think I have illustrated the difference in outlook between the soldier and the airman. What would our *Accidental Warrior* Geoffrey Picot have thought of the 'peggy' airmen who didn't want to go on muster parade?

I am basing my theory on the particular rather than the general, which may be mischievous, so let me quote one small incident which I believe to be typical of the Army officer/man relationship. For almost a year in 1949/50 I commanded a radio troop in BAOR, which was approximately the same length of time I spent with 108 MU. In 1953 I was driving my car through Otley in Yorkshire when I was held up for some reason. A man rushed across the road to make himself known to me. It was one of my ex-national service signalmen from BAOR, Sleightholme by name. Had I, as an Erk, seen one of my officers three years later, would I have done the same? No, I would probably not have even recognised him.

Widening the field even further, the battle between technology and leadership has spread into everyday life. Leadership has been banished in favour of the computer and science. The modern world of management is wedded to these two gods, plus money. I am old-fashioned enough to believe that schooled and educated leadership is vital to mankind's survival. If leadership is left solely to man (not nature), it results in the worst elements coming forward as expounded so well in *Lord of the Flies*. Why

128

is it that the natural leader in the school is, more often than not, the aggressive mischief-maker? But once this aggression has been harnessed, then this leadership can produce the finest possible results – Andy Macnab of *Bravo Two Zero*.

The inseparable twins, leadership and loyalty; without one, the other cannot exist. Dirty words in this 'Age of Political Correctness' – with apologies to Arthur Bryant. Look back fifty years to both sides of the coin, Hitler the evil leader, sweeping Europe before him, then Churchill with his inspirational leadership'. What would have been the outcome without him? Democracy leads to anarchy, whether it be nation, family or anything else; there are so many voices that cohesion is lost. Sooner or later, a Saddam Hussain will emerge from Bongo Bongo land, armed with technology, and will run amok. He will practise a doctrine of divide and conquer, and hey presto he will achieve his objective. Is there not a danger that the world will succumb to his evil leadership? Will the counter-balance be found if society has eliminated the essential ingredient? Do you wonder that I sometimes fear for my grandchildren?

I must return to the problem in hand.

When to pack up or when to go on? I was still in a muddle. Changing course is a difficult path to tread, the known versus the unknown. How far should the track divide before the politician resigns, or the Nazi general rebels – resulting in his destruction? My dilemma was not of these proportions, and I had not analysed the facts in my mind as I have now, all these years later. But I had reached a stage of knowing that things were not right.

Just one more push was essential to make me DO SOMETHING about myself. John had talked about a commission in the Army when we first met, but there the matter rested. Some months later a letter from my mother contained a little of that invaluable ingredient 'feedback'. John had written home and said that 'Harvey seems to lack ambition'. Willy-nilly, some action became necessary.

John had done some spade work for me. Yes, pulling strings, and some might declare this to be deplorable, but it is what happened. It rested with me to start the ball rolling by submitting an application to my own commanding officer. I could not apply for a place at an Army OCTU direct from the RAF, so I had to transfer from RAF to Army. This was the gist of my plea. My RAF CO told me to obtain a statement from the Army to say that they were prepared to accept me. Back to John who arranged an interview for me at GHQ Middle East. I duly marched in to see a Colonel who took a look at me, had a little polite conversation, and said Yes, he would make a recommendation. Armed with this in writing I returned to my own CO, and he approved the transfer. All I now had to do was wait a few weeks while the wheels turned, then on 30 April 1942 I was discharged from the RAF. I had one day as a civilian in Cairo, then reported for enlistment as a Trooper in the RAC. (And what do you think? The digits of my Army personal number added up to the same total as my RAF number – 28 I think. There had to be some significance in this coincidence.)

I wonder how many of us knew what we were doing; I am not sure I did. My CO was probably saying good riddance to bad rubbish, but the Army was buying a pig in a poke. Such was life!

That is the end of the RAF story, but the war was still on, and I was not deceased. It would be unfair to leave my reader at that stage in 1942, so to complete the tale, I continue. However, if you feel that enough is enough, stop here!

Chapter 11

TEACHING GRANDMOTHER

You will have noted my interest in teaching and that I was quite seriously thinking about becoming a schoolmaster after the war. I feel strongly about teaching, and for this reason I am going to divert from my main theme and wander down a side road. If you, my reader, find yourself bored by this excursion, turn round in this gateway and return to the main road at the next chapter.

During the process of trying to decide upon a career I was taken by an aunt to a lawyer's office in Guildford High Street. He was a kindly gentleman and conjured up interest, but not a calling. During our conversation he pointed to a wall covered with most impressive looking books and delivered his pronouncement: 'All the information is there; you do not need to know it by heart, but you must be able to put your finger to the appropriate page when needs demand.'

These words seem to me to be particularly relevant from a teaching point of view.

The human brain is the most complex and efficient computer ever invented, and I am convinced its memory section plays the main role in character building. Take a human life up to the age of seventy, arbitrarily discount the first, say, four years and we are left with a life span of some sixty-six years, times 365 days, times say sixteen wakeful hours, times sixty minutes. All this adds up to 23,147,600 units of one minute. Let us stop at that before going on to seconds. Say the human brain experiences some event, conversation or other occurrence each minute, then the human memory has 23,147,600 such events to record and remember. But it doesn't. It selects just a manageable few, and it is on that selection that character is built. In my teens I must have entered many rooms occupied by strangers, friends and relations, but I have no recollection of those encounters. Not withstanding that, I did remember that lawyer and just one of the sentences he spoke. My own computer registered that remark as being significant to ME, and so it stored it. Having stored it in my computer, it influenced my life thereafter. My aunt's memory was bombarded with the same sentence, but it was of no significance to her so it was rejected and forgotten.

The human being, having inherited the broad basis of character at birth, then selects experiences upon which his character is built. Provided the teacher can 'get through' to the child then the teacher has provided a seed bed in the child's mind which will nurture all the 'right' seeds. The parent, particularly the mother, has the same gift by virtue of parenthood, suckling, and early training of the child. How important teaching is.

I am not up to date with the modern approach to teaching but I can see no tangible evidence of the above line of thought being applied. If teachers are not 'shown the light' then there is little hope of practising their vocation efficiently.

In my old age, my interests still survive, and if I bother to think, I can trace the sparks which ignited the fires to some conversation, some individual, something I had seen or heard, many years ago. I can hope that these interests will provide me with food through my octogenarian and nonagenarian years.

You met JDS in Chapter 2, and I thank him as many times as I have had years for the music I enjoy – and there would be worse things in life than leaving it to the strains of a Mahler song. His legacy was as valuable as anything else I have gained in my life, and it is therefore right that I should explore the anatomy of his gift. Had he taught me science instead of CV, I am sure I would not have been a duffer. He had enthusiasm. It was not confined to his voice; it was in his hands and his whole being. It was infectious.

Let us now carry my argument one stage further. If my thesis is correct, and that which is remembered over the long term helps to form the character, then I would submit that the teacher's objective should be to make full use of this phenomenon. Oh yes, he will say, that is what I do, but I would disagree, not because of personal deficiency, but because of idiotic teaching policies introduced in the sixties by the intellectuals; intellectuals who assess all other peoples' drive and desire from their own standards. There is a world of difference between teaching children who WANT to learn (generally speaking, the offspring of responsible and often educated parents) from those who DO NOT want to learn (generally speaking, the offspring of uneducated, often unemployed parents).

Suppose Mr Ivebeen Everywhere delivers a lecture on his latest venture. At the first talk, 500 education theorists who devised the new teaching methods attend, sit in chairs and lap up every word. At the second talk 500 football fans are pressed to attend because somebody thinks they ought to know about Never Land. Our lecturer divides them up into groups of fifty so that each group can do a project on what he might have discovered in this distant place. He circulates round the groups, and at the end of one hour not a single football fan has learned a thing about Never Land.

This scenario, though perhaps exaggerated, is little different from the classroom of unactivated children; they will never learn anything by sitting round in groups.

I respectfully suggest that curiosity plays a major part in a child's absorption of knowledge. If he is curious, he wants to know, and the process of wanting to know makes the answer, when discovered, more likely to stick. From this I argue that the more any teacher can tickle the curiosity of a child, the more likely the child will be to learn. Mind you, this is difficult to apply in practice in some subjects – after all, why WANT to know that seven times eight equals fifty-six? However, with a bit of imagination, the teaching of many subjects can be contrived as a question-and-answer kaleidoscope.

So much rests with the individual teacher, and there is certainly a fresh wind blowing through education at the present time; but I should be surprised if teachers' training has changed much from the time not long ago when I had a conversation with a young teacher who had recently qualified. I asked her what teaching practice she had received during her training, and now that she was at an actual school, was her performance supervised? Did her headmistress or some senior member of the staff come round and attend her classes from time to time, and give advice? The answer on both counts was negative. This appalled me. How can a teacher learn the art of imparting knowledge if she is not given practice in the classroom? To expect a young teacher to maintain discipline and impart knowledge in front of a lot of children for a forty-minute period without knowing the techniques of how to handle them is little short of cruelty.

At this point, I must revert to my army experience. Again, I am out of date, it is over thirty years since I hung up my uniform but I suspect that the intervening period has added to, rather than subtracted from, what I am about to say. I speak of the Army, but my remarks apply equally to the other two Services. I have absolutely no doubt in my mind that the British Army is every bit as efficient as any other organisation anywhere in the world, not only in its sheer professional capacity, but in its administration and man-management.

If this is so, then one must ask why. Who trains these men? Answer: for the most part, the Army itself. It is therefore logical to ask if Army training methods are not as good as, if not better than, others in the country. I suggest they are, and speak from personal experience as both learner and imparter of knowledge.

For two years I was an instructor in the Signal Wing of the School of Infantry in Hythe, (it removed to Warminster in the 1970s). I arrived with little knowledge of teaching; my odd talk or lecture to troops in the past had been adequate; but I had no experience of the finer points, or of how to go about preparing material for a lesson. I was therefore despatched on a five-day 'Method of Instruction' course. During this five days I was taught the techniques of teaching, collation of the information to be taught, marshalling it into sequence, format of teaching period, i.e. introduction, explanation, demonstration, imitation, criticism, and summary at the end. There were mnemonics to remind one of the sequences. Question-and-answer technique, examination technique, avoidance of mannerism and all aspects of standing in front of thirty men and teaching them something, and last but not least, the importance of capturing the interest of the class at the beginning of the instructional period. The classic 'howler' introduction at that time was, 'What we are going on with this morning is . . .'.

Teaching aids. A subject in itself. Great stress was made on their importance, and we were encouraged to develop our own, anything from a complex sectional model of a piece of apparatus to a ball of string used for demonstrating some simple theoretical principle. Every time I had a

135

bath I would lie there trying to think out something new! A visible presentation by an aid can illustrate a point far better than a thousand words.

Having ploughed through this basic stuff for the first two days, we were then called upon to give teaching practices. Starting with a ten-minute talk we graduated to longer periods on specific subjects. At the end of each talk, the other students would criticise, then the instructor would deliver his judgement. At the end of the five days we had learned a lot and had been assessed doing the actual job.

I returned to Hythe, knowing what I was about, and armed with the self-confidence essential for any instructor. But my training did not end there. During the whole of my two years at the Signal Wing I would expect to see my Commanding Officer or Chief Instructor attend my class from time to time. During an instructional period, the door at the back of the classroom would open and one of the two officers would quietly enter, take a seat, listen to me for ten or fifteen minutes, then withdraw. If he had any points to raise on my own or my students' performance, I would subsequently be summoned into his presence and told about it.

That is not the end of my Hythe story. I had been equipped with the wherewithal to turn me into an instructor, and it was now my turn to pass on my skills to my students – junior officers and NCOs. We were teaching Regimental Signallers to be instructors when they returned to their units at the end of the twelve-week course. The first half of the course was devoted to teaching the knowledge they would be required to pass on, then the second half was teaching them the teaching skills necessary to put their subjects across. This took the form of a prolonged method of instruction course as outlined above. Each student had no less than ten actual teaching practices, starting with one of ten minute, progressing through twenty-minute to a final forty-minute session. We, as instructors, sat in on these practices, criticised, praised and generally steered the students to better things.

The subject matter we were required to teach was also already laid down, so that a uniform syllabus was passed on. Had this not been so, wildly differing targets would have been achieved. Take one subject and fifty teachers, turn them loose and compare what has been taught at the end of a term, and I guarantee some of the results would be as different as chalk from cheese. Teachers should be given parameters within which to concentrate.

What a first-class system; and against this, do you wonder that I was disappointed, to say the least, when I received the answer I did from that novice teacher. Had I asked this young teacher's headmistress why she had not visited the classroom to check on her young recruit, I feel sure I would have been told that lack of time prevented it. To this I would have replied 'Rubbish'; it is not a matter of time but of priorities, and guiding a young teacher is top priority.

The easiest excuse in the world is 'Not to have time'. When I later became Chief Instructor in a Training Regiment, I had to MAKE myself go round the classrooms. There was always something more pressing to do – even if it was only reading the newspaper!

Novice teachers need all the help they can get from their seniors when they first join a school. It must be a daunting experience to stand up in front of a class of rowdy twelve-year-olds for the first time. How can teachers be expected to maintain discipline in the face of a couple of trouble makers if they have not been taught how to deal with such a situation? (How any teacher is supposed to keep order when pupils are sitting round tables, half of them with their backs to what is going on, is something I cannot understand. What a gift to the 'mucker-abouters' – and if I know little boys, most of them are just that – with little intention of learning, particularly from a 'cissy woman teacher'. After all, the hard core of future criminals is in the class somewhere, and the teacher should

137

be equipped for dealing with the worst. Only one trouble maker in a class, and the rest follow like sheep.) I hope every young teacher reads *Lord of the Flies*. Is it the slightest bit surprising that one reads in the newspapers of teachers living in fear? I suggest they would stand a better chance if only they were given the rudimentary skills necessary to practise their trade, (and the classroom organised as it used to be). Furthermore, a higher percentage of male teachers are needed to keep the little male horrors in order.

There is a strong affinity between acting and teaching. Both require the showman's skill; both are extroverts, they use voice and gestures to put their message across. The only real difference is that the actor is not using his own words, whereas the teacher extemporises. Both are entertainers. If the actor requires training at RADA, so does the teacher. I am not talking about the higher echelons of teaching. Let the professors exchange their knowledge in their own way – to the lesser mortals the very subject of their dissertation would probably be as dull as ditchwater. No. I am talking about run-of-the-mill teaching, at the bottom of the scale – so far at the bottom, in fact, that even more guile is needed by the teacher to make his offering palatable to the least intelligent. One can go so far as to say that the more disadvantaged (to use that horrible modern expression) the child, the more skilled the teaching required.

Let me now divert for a few moments to give some valuable advice on cheating. From as early as I can remember, I suffered from a roving eye. Whenever I was supposed to be doing something, my eyes would circumnavigate my surroundings, lapping up non-essential detail instead of attending to the job in hand. This habit strayed into the classroom, and the first real manifestation that I can recall was at the end of my first term at school. We were doing a written test – or call it an exam, that sounds better – and the subject was geography. The question was something to do with cold places, and the correct answer was probably the Alps or

Himalayas. However, I was stumped. Then the roving eye came into operation, I detected a word in my neighbour's answer and seized upon it to prove my knowledge. Alas, his answer was wrong, and furthermore, his spelling of Iceland was Cieland. My spelling was identical. The moral of the story is that if you are going to cheat, then make sure that the provider of your inspiration is not giving you 'duff gen'.

Many years later, still suffering from the same complaint, I was sitting a classroom test – nothing serious, and no promotion depended upon it. The questions were of the short answer type, so there was a problem of remembering the string of one word answers at the right moment when called upon to do so. Ten minutes thought could have provided the whole lot, but only the two minutes allowed caused a problem. Such was the case when I remembered all but one. The roving eye supplied the full house. Now should I or should I not have made use of this little windfall? I KNEW the answer, but it escaped me at that moment. I used it.

That it not quite the end of the story; if it had been, I would have forgotten all about it, but the worst happened. I achieved top marks of the whole class! My laurels were not justified, and ever since then it has played on my conscience that I cheated.

What a Johnny Know All, you may say at this stage. Don't get me wrong. I am not trying to pretend that I am the very paragon of a teacher. I am not. Just reasonably average. Something I would not have been had I not been taught the skills through a first class system.

I will finish this diversion with a quotation from Thomas Hardy's *Tess of the d'Urbervilles*, Chapter 3:

'All these young souls were passengers in the Durbeyfield ship –
entirely dependent on the judgement of the two Durbeyfield adults
for their pleasures, their necessities, their health, even their existence.
If the heads of the Durbeyfield household chose to sail into difficulty,

disaster, starvation, disease, degradation, death, thither were these half-dozen little captives under hatches compelled to sail with them – six helpless creatures, who had never been asked if they wished for life on any terms, much less if they wished for it on such hard conditions as were involved in being of the shiftless house of Durbeyfield'

One hundred years on, and to the end of time, there will be no change. One parent, two parent, multi-parent families, a percentage will always be the same. What a responsibility teachers have, to counterbalance such parents in-built deficiency in the human race. I admire them for taking on the burden, and ask only that they be given all the tools to make their task the easier.

So much for my theories on teaching, you can now return to the main road and follow my Erk's progress.

Chapter 12

MAKING TRACKS

Drive Training
"Grant" tank

Out of the blue, into khaki.

A black beret instead of a blue forage cap. I fancied myself in it.

Abbassia Barracks. After nine months of sand and tent bashing it was wonderful to be in a building again. These were peacetime barracks, two storey affairs with wide columned balconies round the central barrack room; hot and cold water, showers, baths, tables and chairs and all mod. cons., all within a well-equipped military establishment complete with mess hall and canteens. Highly civilised. There was only one small snag. Bed bugs. I had met fleas and animal lice in my time, but never bed bugs. This was a new experience. The buildings were alive with them; they liked the hot climate and families of them lived in every nook and cranny of the walls. If one poked about in the tiny gaps in the masonry with a matchstick one would unearth the little beasts. They lived there during the daytime, but at night, when the lights went out they sallied forth as an army, marching in line abreast to find luscious human blood. Happening to slaughter one after such a feast it would leave a nasty bloody mess. Soldiery solved the problem. We stood each leg of the bed in a tin of water. Bed bugs could not swim, and we thereby enjoyed peaceful nights.

Later, in India, where our sleeping mode was on charpoys, these harboured bed bugs to an equal extent, so the same tactic was used. A charpoy is a wooden frame bed with coir 'springs', and the bugs nestled in all the wood joints. Army camps were equipped with large vats into which whole charpoys could be dunked in boiling water – no doubt producing a brew of boiled bug soup!

I found that I fitted in well with the RAC Troopers. There was a higher percentage of slightly older men, and even though I was still immature myself, I got on better with older company.

Abbasia Barracks. Writing home.

Life became orderly again. In the RAF we had come and gone much as we liked without muster parades. Here in Abbassia the ringing tones of 'Fall in outside' occurred quite frequently to no resentment, and I suppose psychologically it was reassuring to know that we were working to an organised régime. I was known to be a potential officer cadet, and I well remember an occasion when we had fallen in outside the barrack block, and the Sergeant called me out of the ranks, telling me to take the squad to wherever it was. Oh dear, how embarrassing! What do I do now? I called them to attention in an apologetic voice, almost adding please at the end of it:

'Right turn, quick march.'

Nobody kept in step and so I murmured 'left right, left right', so quietly that nobody could hear. As for the halt when we reached our destination, it was like a machine gun; giving the order on the correct foot did not enter into it.

I have no idea why I was in the Tank Corps, but having got there, they had to do something with me while waiting to go to India for my officer training. So . . . more training, for tank crew duties.

I was virtually starting again from scratch. The skills required were entirely different from those of an RAF rigger. To start with I could not even drive, and this led to some excitement. The first time I ever sat in a driving seat for real, was in a Stuart tank (a Honey tank), and I learned the basic manipulation of controls on this machine. I am not sure that it was the ideal arrangement, but I was willing, and I put all the beef I had into the job, and when I say beef, I mean it. I believe the weight on the clutch pedal was well over 20 pounds, so one braced one's backside against the seat and pushed hard. Doing this to the time of a double de-clutch was exhilarating! Bodyweight forward and into neutral, change foot, press the accelerator to the sound of take off noise from the back as the engine went into maximum rev, a two-handed wrestle with the gear lever on the right, barking one's knuckles on the engine casing only a couple of inches from the handle, back onto the clutch; then the whole machine either came to a total halt, or shot off across the desert at an uncontrolled speed. Steering was fun too; in the absence of a steering wheel one yanked on a pair of levers, one either side; this altered the drive through the differential so that one track moved faster than the other. If one pulled one of the leavers fully back then that track stopped and the other accelerated so that the tank went into gyration. There were about four or five of us learners in each tank, so the others quickly wrote out their wills and testaments before I had time to upset the vehicle completely. The Grant tank was even bigger and better, with an aero engine at the back. When I eventually graduated to a three-tonner, I found the controls so light that I almost put the clutch pedal through the floor and the gear lever through the windscreen. It was all good fun and I thoroughly enjoyed making tracks.

In the classroom we learned the theoretical side of how vehicles worked, and there were fascinating cut-away demonstration models of all the components. We had to know the driver's maintenance schedule too, so we graduated as small-time grease monkeys.

Radio communication is all important in tank battle, so quite a lot of time was spent on this subject. The 19 set had recently been introduced and was the main tank set; in addition to the primary set used for communicating on the regimental net, It contained a revolutionary device for the time, a little secondary 'B' set, operating on VHF, for communication between individual tanks of the troop/squadron. We had to be proficient at not only operating the set(s) but also elementary fault finding. Being valve sets, these were the most likely components to pack up, so each set had a set of spare valves and, as an operator, one was expected to be able to diagnose a faulty valve and replace it.

To sit in front of a wireless set and operate it was one thing, but to communicate between tanks in battle was not the same thing at all. Not a mobile phone conversation with aunty! Operating procedures were all important; first of all one had to establish communications on the chosen frequency, then maintain communications however difficult the conditions on the air and in the tank. There were cut and dried procedures which we had to know instinctively; it was no good having to THINK at the vital moment – the reaction had to be instinctive – which meant a lot of practice in the classroom, on the training ground and on live manoeuvres:

'Hello BOLO, COMO calling. How do you hear me?'

'Strength three, interference strength five.'

Conditions were difficult.

There was another factor of equal importance. Enemy interception. It was hammered into us at every opportunity that the enemy was listening and could gain intelligence from the slightest deviation from the laid down operating procedures. For example a morse transmission ended with a group AR (. – . – .). Now if the operator put in an idiosyncratic extra dot at the end (. – . – . .), this could be registered by the enemy as belonging to Trooper X. The enemy heard this being used in, shall we say, the Tobruk area, then the next time he heard it, it was at Benghazi. A piece in a jigsaw puzzle which, together with information gleaned elsewhere confirmed that the Regiment to which Trooper X belonged had moved and was ready for deployment against him at Benghazi. Radio interception played an enormous part in the war.

The world knows what the Allies gained from breaking Enigma, but they are not so aware of the importance that radio security played in the everyday life of every soldier operating a radio set. As I said, we practised and practised so that procedures came to us automatically, without thought.

Other instruction included gunnery, and a current affairs session each week.

This must have been the time when I first met ABCA, to which reference is occasionally made in modern journalism. A policy had been adopted whereby all commanding officers would be responsible for keeping their soldiers up to date in current affairs, and the machinery for doing this would be a weekly instructional period conducted by officers to the men under their command. The subject of each week's talk/discussion was laid down in a double page ABCA leaflet, issued from the UK. These leaflets were compiled with a strong left wing slant, and were partly responsible for Labour winning the election in 1945. The perpetrators did their work well, and the seed was being sown on fertile ground; we all, to a greater or lesser extent, were left wing, and I remember being most impressed with a report on the Russian 'Five Year Plan' in a book which I bought while at Abu Sueir, *Europe since the War.*

I was at Abbassia when General Montgomery took over command, and it had an immediate impact. His leadership filtered down to the lowest rank; we marched more upright and our eyes were brighter. Even though we had no direct contact with him, his presence was felt all the way down the chain of command.

The situation in the Middle East became fraught in the summer of 1942. Rommel was close to the Delta so all pumps were manned. We trainees at Abbassia were called forward to man additional tank reinforcements. Because I was quite good on the radio, I was sent as a squadron commanders operator. Alas, it was not quite as easy as in the classroom, but I was saved. My posting to India came through so I departed in a blaze of glory instead of ignominy.

A passage to India, and a very comfortable one at that: three weeks of luxury with nothing to do but laze on a ship. She was a comparatively small passenger/cargo, with only very few of us aboard, of all ranks. I had a cabin, and it was all so different from the *Eastern Prince*, and I got on well with my fellow passengers, whatever the rank. Off we tootled down the Red Sea. For some reason or another there was a delay at Aden and I spent a week in a transit camp at Khormaksar. This gave me time to explore the colony and to inspect the whalebones at the Queen of Sheba's wells. The huge catchment tanks were capable of holding millions of gallons of water, dating back to the time when Aden enjoyed a rainfall. One way and another this was a delightful sojourn – and put me in a good mood!

Landfall in India. Bombay, and what an introduction to that country. A majestic setting with the Gateway of India backed by the Taj Mahal Hotel, as the King Emperor saw it back in 1911.

I think I fell in love with the country from that moment; no doubt my stepfather's continual reminiscences of his service in India had something to do with it. The place was not strange, I felt that I knew it already. I made my resolve. I would see as much of this country as I possibly could.

I found myself waiting for about six weeks in Bombay in a transit camp out at Colaba, so I was able to explore the city, discover the magnificent Victoria Railway Station, sip *nimbo pani* at cafés. and absorb the atmosphere of this teaming city. We were close to the sea at Colaba, so there was sea bathing – and on one occasion a head – attached to a body – bobbed past a few yards out. A drowned seaman. At night, attendance at the open-air cinema. I went to *New Moon* twice, listened to Nelson Eddy and Jeanette MacDonald singing their hearts out beneath a canopy of stars. I was content with the choice I had made even though I had not yet faced reality of service in India. I returned to Bombay five months later for a week's leave as an officer cadet, thus carrying higher status. I divided time between the Swimming Club and the paradise-like beach at Juhu, Santa Cruz; a forty-five minute journey by train to the north, a tonga ride, then a virgin beach with miles of sand and gentle rollers coming in, backed by palm trees, with just the occasional native fisherman's hut. A few years ago there was a television programme about this place; horrors, it had become the home of Gurus, and looked like

147

suburbia. Another worthwhile expedition was to the Elephanta Caves. These caves had huge statues of Hindu gods carved from the rocks, in great underground caverns. They were located some little distance from Bombay, reached in a couple of hours by boat.

The odd excursion enlivened the proceedings. I was detailed for an escort party, taking a naughty soldier back to his Regiment at Jubblepore; it was a journey of over twelve hours by train, up through the Western Ghats, two engines tugged the heavily loaded train up the steep escarpment, with glimpses down onto the coastal plain. Magic. Arrival at Jubblepore coincided with a Hindu festival; after dark, candles were alight in every window and alcove.

To Belgaum, down in the south, halfway to Bangalore, to the OTS (Officer Training School) where I had the misfortune (or was it fortune) to find myself in an eleven man section, of whom eight were commandos who had marched out of Burma in the withdrawal. We had a reputation to keep up; we had to be first up the mountain or across the obstacle. My little legs worked overtime. And I am sure we carried heavier backpacks than the rest of the cadets.

After three months at Belgaum, during which time we had been selected to an arm of the service, we moved on for further specialist training; in my case to the STC (Signal Training School) for four months at Mhow. Why signals? I don't know, other than that I had particularly enjoyed the signal part of my RAC training:

We were destined for the Indian Army, serving with Indian troops. Throughout our training at both OTS Belgaum and STC Mhow, we had to learn to speak Urdu. We had formal tuition and private coaching, and we had to pass an exam before we were commissioned.

Mhow was a good station, up in the Central Provinces. It was situated at over 3,000 feet, so the climate was reasonable. It was served by a narrow gauge railway onto which one changed at Kandwa Junction. Our mode of transport at the cantonment was bicycle, and it was surprising how far we ventured on these boneshakers. A popular destination was the swimming pool about five miles away. Another was the Patal Pani water fall – a comparatively modest affair of 100 feet, reached by cycling down the railway track. Rather further afield, but still by bicycle, was a much bigger fall with a sheer drop of over 300 feet. The sublime trip which I made on a subsequent stay at Mhow was to the old Mogul city of Mandu, about ninety miles away. This was unbelievable, still in a good state of preservation, covering about five miles square, with wonderful Mogul buildings. The city was on the edge of the escarpment, and two pavilions were built right on the lip, with views down to the south over the plain far below. What a site, what a place; if it were not for my photographs, I would think that I had imagined the whole thing.

The signal training covered all the subjects to be expected, operation of the different radio sets in use at the time, morse up to about fifteen words a minute, morse and voice procedures, line laying, telephones and exchanges, plus all the background theory so that we had a good basic knowledge of what we were doing. One of the Indian officers on the cadre was to become one of (if not the) youngest Indian Brigadier: Baghat Singh.

On 6 June 1943, I sprouted my first pip, just six days before my twenty-first birthday. I was now a wartime officer in the Indian Army.

Chapter 13

FULFILMENT

An officer . . . and gentleman, I hope. In embryo form.

With still two years of the war to run, I have no intention of submitting my reader to a blow by blow account of the remaining 700 days. Relax! I will just latch onto a few less usual aspects of life as I experienced them.

The first is ciphers. You will have realised from my last chapter that I have a slight bee in my bonnet about radio security; this is more to do with subsequent events than instruction when with the RAC, but it is important, nevertheless.

I had made a conscious effort to be commissioned into Indian Signals, but I had no say in my first posting to GHQ India. Why they should have selected a totally green young subaltern to reinforce the General Staff Intelligence (Signals) at Delhi, I do not know; but they did, and I now found myself in a world of ciphers and radio security. For the first few weeks, to get the feel of the thing, I was sat down – with the one other recruit – and told to do a bit of code breaking. Substitution and transposition was explained to us and we were then given pieces of encoded text to 'break'. All quite simple, and it introduced us to the principles on which the whole cipher system is based. Coupled with this, we were shown intercepted plain language radio messages which contained breaches of security; and it was explained how these – very small in themselves – telltale minor breaches helped to complete a far bigger picture which could lead to the enemy having pre-knowledge about an impending operation.

'The enemy is listening' . . . to every radio transmission.

Meanwhile I was revelling in New Delhi; with its Lutyens Secretariat Building, Baker's Viceregal Lodge, the Council Chamber, Connaught Circus, and Kingsway with the statue of King George V; I thought it the most wonderful city I had ever seen.

A month of this then I was shuttled round India, down to the south to Madras and Bangalore for I am not sure what; but I filled in time with a fantastic visit to what I worked out to be the Javadi Hills near Jalapet Junction. I was in camp there and, to the south, an intriguing plateau rose above the plain. Curiosity got the better of me; with another fellow we hired bicycles and set off down dusty tracks through native villages to this mirage. Leaving the machines leaning against a tree, we climbed up into wonderland. It was green and fresh with glades running through the trees, complete with butterflies and birds. I have no photographs or other record of this excursion and sometimes wonder if it really happened, but I'm sure it did. The hills are on the map, and it must be true. As for Bangalore, to me it was the home of white ants; little encrusted channels ran up every wall, and if one knocked away a section, it revealed these teeming termites, scuttling up and down.

It was August 1943. Rangoon had fallen in March of the previous year and the old Burma Army had marched some 800 miles up the Irrawaddy valley and through the mountains to Imphal (nine of the men I was with at

Belgaum). Until now, the old Command had included Bengal and Eastern India as well as the operational front. It was now being split into Eastern Command and 14th Army. Currently located in Calcutta, General Slim moved Headquarters out of the city centre to Barrackpore, and it was at this stage that I joined them – at a time of serious flooding in Bengal, with the army committed to flood relief duties.

A more than twenty four hour train journey brought me from Madras to Calcutta where I started in business for the first time with my newly learned skills. I had access to the cipher strongroom. We were responsible for distribution of all cipher material which was kept in a large basement room in HQ building. It was located behind a heavy iron grill door which was padlocked.

One morning my boss and I went to the strongroom only to find that the padlock was locked but not engaged over the hasp. Anyone could have entered during the previous evening and during the night. Oh dear, dog house. I was guilty. If somebody had got in, it was possible that the whole of the ciphers for the operational area, Line of Communication back to GHQ India and indeed War Office, were compromised. My poor boss. He had a dreadful decision to make. Should he declare a possible compromise which would have caused the whole of the war plans to be thrown into jeopardy, or say nothing. We worked out that it was highly unlikely that anyone had got in, nothing was missing and so he made his decision – say nothing. He saved my bacon, and I learned a lesson.

The sorting out process of the two Commands led to part of Eastern Command being sent down to Tollygung to the south of the city. One might class Tollygung as a mini Hampstead millionaires row, complete with race course, golf course and the Rhani's Palace. This latter was the Headquarters building, an imposing edifice with large entrance hall and grand staircase leading up from the front door. At mezzanine level the stair forked back on itself to right and left. Two doors faced the two

152

secondary flights. Enter, and behold the most sumptuous double bathroom. Such was life for her Ladyship, the Rhani.

Returning to ciphers, Delhi was the main cipher distribution centre, so every month a courier guard of two or three officers, armed with pistols, would make the twenty-four hour journey to Delhi and back by train. The ciphers were very bulky and carried in large leather panniers. An enjoyable excursion.

Life in the fleshpots of Calcutta was perfect. If Bombay was teaming, Calcutta was double teaming with humanity. It was not good for a young officer who should have been taking a more active part in the war; however, I did not grumble and made the most of the Saturday Club dances, thé dansant at the Great Eastern Hotel, lunch at the same establishment of bekite fish and tartar sauce to the accompaniment of a palm court orchestra.

Then there was entertainment at the cinema and by the Calcutta Symphony Orchestra. Liesel Stary was a professional pianist; she played the *Grieg Concerto*, and her star turn was the *Warsaw Concerto* which she recorded for HMV at their Dum Dum factory, to the north of the city.

By October 1943, 14th Army had established Headquarters at Comilla, some 200 miles to the East of Calcutta, on the east side of the Brahamaputra. To get there involved a train journey to Goalundo, a ferry for about seventy-four miles down the river to Chandpur, then another fifty miles by train. This was to be my destination. I was dogsbody in the GSI(s) branch to Major Eric Austerfield, and two Captains, Paul Buroughs and Maurice Brown. The latter was king of the ciphers with his strongroom similar to that in Barrackpore. Courier duties were still on the menu, but now we had the extra bit of the journey to Calcutta. More swanning around.

The cipher books were stacked on shelves in the strongroom like a library. A physical check would be made against the inventory on a regular basis; but books were not necessarily removed from the shelves. One day we took down a large volume from the shelf, it looked alright but when we opened the cover, there were no pages! It had been eaten hollow by white ants. It gave us some amusement to record on the destruction certificate 'Consumed by white ants'.

I was at Comilla at the time of the Japanese attack in the Arakan when 7 Division Admin Box was overrun. The cipher office was overrun and the chief cipher officer was killed. It was feared that all ciphers might have been compromised. However, when the officer's body was found the vital pieces of secret equipment were still in his pocket, so an enormous crisis was averted.

There were quite a number of outlying independent forces operating in the theatre, and they had to be equipped with ciphers. All supply to these forces was by air, so this included new cipher keys and pads. It was the practice for men from HQ to go on these flights to help push the stuff out of the Dakotas over the dropping zone. Shortly after I left 14th Army HQ, Maurice went on such a trip. The aircraft crashed and he was killed. Such is chance in war. I was the one going to an operational unit, but had I stayed at GSI(s) it might easily have been my turn for a flight. I had shared my bamboo basher (hut) with Maurice for nearly six months, he was a devoted family man, with a photograph of his wife always beside him. How she must have grieved when she was told of his death.

Before leaving the subject of ciphers and radio security, I will mention one other event. Everybody knows of the phantom invasion force in the south-east corner of England in 1944, but I wonder how many know that a similar, though smaller, operation was carried out in Burma. Once conceived, it was planned in detail by Paul Buroughs, but after I had departed GSI(s). It was designed to deceive the Japanese about the crossing of the Chindwin. It involved operating a whole phantom Corps radio network to make it appear that they were advancing in a certain direction when, in fact, they were moving to attack on a different front, under radio silence. A calculated number of enciphered messages were sent over the various radio links according to a realistic pattern, and the odd voice radio transmission provided misleading information. This deception plan, together with other scraps of information leaked to the Japanese by various means, contributed very considerably to the success of the operation.

Came the day in the summer of 1944 when I was posted. I took a fortnight's leave and went to Kashmir with Geoffrey Sheath. James Hilton must have been to Kashmir to gain the inspiration for writing *Lost Horizon*. Kashmir was Shangri-La. Everything about it. The Dal Lakes, the mountains, the Jellum river, the shikaras, the town of Srinagar, walnut beautifully carved into every conceivable shape, hand-painted papiermaché trays and objects, and the exquisite embroidery. I have a twenty foolscap page typed record of that leave, together with photographs, and Younghusband's book on Kashmir and the surrounding mountains (after moving to Hythe, I met a relative of his who lived just down the road from us). It was all marvellous. In some ways I would like to re-visit, but it would never be the same, and anyway it has been ravished by war for so many years.

On this trip too, it was quite interesting to experience another piece of geography. On our way to Kashmir by taxi we had to cross the foothills of the Himalayas before descending to the Jellum river. It was a dull day, and as we climbed the 6,000 feet on the south side of the hills, the weather closed in and it started to rain; by the time we reached the top, the rain had progressed through sleet to sloppy snow and there were signs of it settling. On the north side as we went down, the snow had settled and was still falling as snow at least 1,000 feet lower down the mountain.

Shangri-La. I did not realise it at the time, but I had found mine in 26 Indian Divisional Signal Regiment, with whom I served for nearly two years, less a gap in the middle when I returned to the UK on leave.

I left all my heavy kit, including my portable gramophone and records, in store in Calcutta, and reported to my new unit down in the Arakan.

Sammy Stead was my commanding officer, born in India, a perfect gentleman and a fluent Urdu speaker. I was posted to 1 Squadron as second in command of 'O' Troop, responsible for manning the signal office. My squadron commander was Len Gregory who was also a fluent Urdu speaker and had tremendous charisma, though not everybody got on with him. I did.

This was a unit of mixed British and Indian ranks, and therefore of quite different character to either a British Battalion serving in India, or a completely Indian Regiment such as the 1st Punjab. There was a mixture of British and Indian right through all ranks; the second in command of the Regiment was an Indian King Commissioned Officer – Lal Hussein – and there were a number of other Indian officers. Shamboo Singh had been educated in England and was more British than the British. Many years later, when I read *The Jewel in the Crown*, poor Kumar took on the persona of Shamboo. How I felt for him. There was a British RSM and his Indian equivalent in the person of the Havildar Major, a Viceroy Commissioned officer: there were British senior NCOs and Indian senior NCOs and so on down the chain of command to BORs and IORs (British other ranks and Indian other ranks). Messing was segregated so that there were British, Hindu, Muslim, and Sikh cookhouses. Individual Troops were composed of single Indian sects, thus Main Div. Radio Troop was Madrassi, while Rear Div. Radio Troop was Muslim. British and Indian signalmen worked alongside one another, so that, for instance, my signal office would be manned by a shift of a mixture of British and Indian of all ranks up to Sergeant. All lived and worked amicably together without any friction and yet, I have little doubt that when partition of India came in 1948, at least one of my men must have been slaughtered by a fellow ex-signalman of 26 Indian Div. Signals. Oh shame.

I remember an early initiation into the officers mess. I happened to mention the gramophone and records which I had left in Calcutta. Interest was shown. What records did I have, and did I know Shostakovich's first symphony? Regrettably, I had never even heard of the gentleman; my taste only ran to such as the *New World Symphony* and Russian music was just about limited to Tchaikovsky's *Piano Concerto*. I was treated to a dissertation on the merits of Shostakovich, and we all made great friends. Within no time at all I had fitted in to the Regiment and became an integral part of it, completely at home with all ranks of both nationalities. Compared with my arrival and reception at some of my postings in future years, this was perfect. The initial impression is so important; a foot placed wrong within the first few days can take a long time to rectify.

RHB with IORs of 'O' Troop
Back row: VV Pillai, Yellapan, Sultan Singh, L/Nk Khadan,
Gopal Menon, Khan Singh, V Perumal, Ramaswany, Michael
Centre row: Jemadhar Daniel, Self, Havildar Subramanaum
Front row: Alwar, Mercellino, Naraynan, Appu Kutty Nair

At some stage within the next few months I was put in charge of an advance party responsible for setting up communications for Main Division in a new location. I duly set about the task with a party of some twenty or thirty men, but we ran out of food! I asked for rations but was told that I had not indented for them so could not have any! I discovered the importance of administration, there was more to signalling than just operating a radio set or pushing messages through the system; body and soul had to be kept together and that required forethought and action. I had learned another lesson.

Some time towards the end of the year I was sent to Sialkot in Northern India for a month's course on Permanent Line construction – telephone poles and all that. It was a journey of over 1,500 miles to get there, first by jeep to Chittagong, then by rail. By this time I was well experienced in Indian rail travel, having covered at least 15,000 miles since my arrival at Bombay just over a year previously. A wonderful way to travel, in four berth compartments into which one bedded down for anything from twenty-four to forty-eight hours (Delhi–Madras). The train would stop for meals. The station would provide a sit-down feast in the 'restaurant', then when we had finished, the train would progress on its way.

The Sialkot course ended three days early. We were near Kashmir so Joe Muggins got to work (I always seemed to be the ringleader at these things). I persuaded another fellow to accompany me to the Kashmir border at Banihal. Enquiries revealed that a bus service ran from Jammu to Srinagar over the Banihal Pass (I had been by the other route, via Murree, in the summer) stopping for the night at the bottom of the pass on the India side. We could stay overnight in the Dak bungalow, travel on by bus to the top of the pass the following day, disembark there and make our own way down on foot back to Banihal for a second night in the bungalow, then return to Jammu the following day by a return bus. An excellent plan. But . . . the first part went according to schedule; we duly got to the top of the pass – where I dropped my camera down many feet of mountain side when the stitching on the leather carrier broke. I recovered it, but the camera opened and I lost the film. We made our way back and had a snug night in the bungalow (bath in a tub by the log fire) and all was fine.

However, during the night there was a heavy snowfall. The pass was blocked. No return bus. Crisis, what to do? There were no other British within hundreds of miles. We touted round the village, using our best Urdu and eventually found an antique three-ton lorry which was going back to Jammu with a load of tree trunks. We could travel on it. There was a log bench across the back of the lorry and we were to sit on this, alongside three Kashmiris. Each had his little *meri ag*. This was 'my little fire': a small pot of burning charcoal which was held on the lap underneath the blanket which enveloped each man, thus keeping him warm. We had no such luxury. We made our perilous way back over about 150 miles of rough mountain road in this fashion. The lorry had a six foot overhang behind the rear wheels, so that our bench at the very back of the vehicle swung out over the abyss when we went round right hand bends; the river was a long way below! It was quite a trip, but worth every minute.

At that time, I could recommend a kill or cure remedy to any nervous car passenger; a drive down from a Himalayan Hill Station at 8,000 feet to the Plain, in an Indian driven taxi. Exhilarating! To start with, the taxi would bear maximum resemblance to a Jalopy with 100,000 on the clock. The roads were metalled but none too wide, and they followed every contour of the mountain side. Having piled into the back of the vehicle the journey would start at break-neck speed down the mountain, braking hard at each corner. Periodically the driver would draw to a sudden halt alongside a small water cascade where a bucket would be found. He would leap out of the car, fill the bucket and chuck the contents at each wheel in turn. Clouds of steam would rise with a loud hissing noise and after two or three dousings the brake drums would be cool enough to start off on the next leg of the journey, to the next water hole.

This experience paid me a dividend on 13 September 1984. My wife and I had driven up to the Gross Glockner and were returning quite late in the evening. Some way down we espied a notice in many languages telling us to test the brakes. We did. They weren't. Fortunately our speed was slow at that point and we came to a halt in a lay-by. What to do? The notice did not tell us, but memory came to the rescue. We detected a small tumble of water, then proceeded to fill two lemonade bottles and pour the contents over the wheels. It worked, and hey presto, after many trips to the tumble, we were able to set off again in the dark.

This excursion to the Gross Glockner leads me back to my first encounter in 1949. In my brand new Austin A70, I toured Europe, taking my Mother on a one-time-only holiday. Our route led us up the mountain late one evening in August.

'We will find somewhere on the way up for the night,' says I, but the further we went the less likely this became. However, there was a small establishment in the saddle below the Eidelweiss Spitze where I bedded down an agitated Mother who longed at that point for nothing better than her own bed in Dorset. At ten o'clock, we were plunged into darkness when the power generator was turned off for the night. Next morning, what a joy. Shortly after sunrise I went up the Eidelweiss Spitze and marvelled at the sight – long before it became one gigantic car park. Few things can equal the early morning sun glinting on the snow-covered peaks, under a clear blue sky, in a particularly magnificent setting. (Tailpiece. Forty years on and my third trip. The Gross Glockner glacier is a filthy black mess,and one parks in a multi-storey car park. Never again, thank you.)

So much for that little diversion; my apologies, and I now continue with the main theme.

I returned to the Regiment, where we were preparing for a seaborne landings down the coast of the Arakan. These were intended to provide air bases for supply of the main force advancing down the Irrawaddy. Our first step was Akyab, but the Japanese departed of their own accord. Our objective was switched to Ramree Island where we had the pleasure of wading ashore on 26 January at Kyaukpu (pronounced Chogpu).

An isolated incident is worth a mention. I had to go up to Chittagong to fetch some vehicles. (We existed on only twelve for a time, to serve the whole of that part of the Regiment located at Divisional headquarters; since this included line laying and despatch rider duties it was a bit of a strain!). The road was built up onto a bund and was unmetalled. There had been rain and it was very slippery. We drove on through the night,

Feb. 95. Ramree landing. Going ashore.

and I was driving the leading jeep.

Suddenly – Help – a herd of elephants crossing the road. BRAKE.

I jammed on the brakes. No elephants. I was driving, but my mind had wandered onto a different plain. I woke up.

It was very lucky that the driver of the vehicle behind me was alert, and that my jeep did not end up in the paddy field at the bottom of the bund. I realised that if I was seeing elephants, then the Indian drivers might be seeing things too. Discretion was the better part of valour. We pulled in to the next military unit we saw and bedded down for the rest of the night.

Incidentally, the American Dodge 15 cwts. were worth their weight in gold. One in ten of them had a winch mounted at the front, and this winch was forever in use. either for pulling other vehicles out of the ditch, or else itself – just unwind the cable and anchor it to a tree. The Dodge

Feb. 95. Ramaree landing. Setting up signal office.

162

heaved itself back onto the road in no time at all.

Finally, I cannot allow Lord Louis Mountbatten's visit to pass unmentioned. He has come in for so much flak from the armchair critics, but I think all of us who were out there know what he did for the Command. He visited our Division, and we were summoned to a clearing in the jungle. He arrived in a Jeep, stood on the bonnet and talked to us as equals. That is what leadership is made of.

It is not my task to tell the history of the war in Burma. The authentic version is told by Field Marshall Sir William Slim in his *Defeat into Victory*. I played my little tiny part in it, and I took over the Main Div. Radio Troop with promotion to Captain, while at Kyaukpu.

Within a few months, my overseas tour was reaching four years and I was due for Python (Permanent repatriation to the UK). I didn't want to lose my ties. I was content in 26. I therefore applied for LILOP (Long leave in lieu of Python) on the understanding that I would return to the Regiment after my leave. In due course my papers came through and I was on my way. I spent VE night in a railway siding at Comilla station, flew home in three days from Karachi, and touched down just outside Yeovil, only twelve miles from home on 31 May.

Chapter 14

REALITY

That is where my Erk's progress should end, but to leave it there would be dishonest and imply a Little Jack Horner situation. It was not like that. I have to admit that retirement from the Army twenty years later was in the rank of . . . Major. All that much progress in twenty years. What happened to Erk? Answer – he operated best when unsupervised.

I had my leave and returned to India, but to my extreme anger I was posted to Ceylon Army Command Signals. I made myself rather unpopular until I was posted back to 26, by that time in Sumatra. Here it was the same mix as before, Sammy Stead, Len Gregory and the Indian troops.

The mix misled me. You may remember a book entitled 'The Singer not the Song' about a priest in Mexico. He was a fine man and the people respected him, not for his religion but for the man he was. In the same way, I mistook 26 for the whole Army. I applied for a regular army commission, attended WOSB (WAR Office Selection Board) in Singapore and was accepted. Within three years of first commissioning, I was posted to Singapore to take up a plum new appointment as the permanent secretary of four Telecommunications Boards and Committees. This was mainly due to Colonel Sammy's recommendation. I was one of about four or five such secretaries operating under the umbrella of the South East Asia Secretariat, headed by Brigadier Dolphin. I was granted the temporary rank of Major. We occupied prestigious offices on the seventh floor of the Cathay Building; my office had a balcony with a view right out across the city and the harbour. I was more or less independent answering, at a fairly remote distance, to the Chief Signal Officer of FARELF (Far East Land Forces), also in Singapore. Two years later, when my tour of duty finished, the Brigadier (Fatty Galwey) said that for the first three months

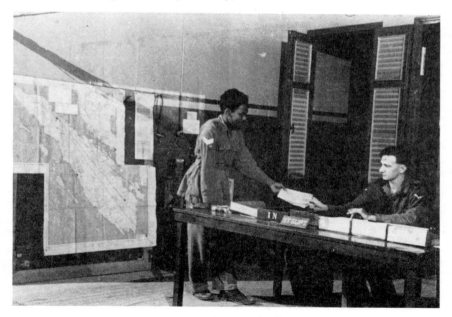

Sumatra, the signal office.

165

he wondered what the cat had brought in, but by the end of my tour he considered me one of the best officers under his command. A complex mixture, and a doubtful auger for the future.

Too late I realised that I should have taken a degree at the end of the war and followed my schoolmaster grandfather s footsteps; it was seven years before I discovered that my initial choice would have been right. I was appointed as an instructor within the Army for two years, and in the course of time I returned to the instructional field for the last few years of my service in charge of a branch of army trade training. The snag was that my priorities were wrong; I wanted to be a teacher first and a soldier second.

There was an ability to reach higher rank, but it was not to be, for reasons I can trace to childhood. As my secondary theme is teaching, this

Sumatra, RHB at a 399 set.

fact is relevant and is, I believe, worthy of further study before the last page is turned.

Tell me to list fifty of my own adult characteristics, then tell me to trace evidence of them back to my earliest awareness. With thought – and honesty – I can do it:

The wandering eye	–	to Cieland;
Interest in history	–	JDS;
Dislike of broken promises	–	to the rector's daughter;
Love for reference books	–	that lawyer in Guildford;
Unsociability	–	to a solitary childhood in Dorset

and so the list goes on, plus a lot more, to pre-memory days. The common denominator is the influence dictated throughout childhood by individuals and circumstances. Many characteristics are inherited but they are built on and modified by grown-ups during childhood.

It was Field Marshall Montgomery who said something to the effect that a person's character is formed by the time the child is five. Thereafter, for the next ten years, this character is built upon, and by the mid teens there is not much anyone can do to change the character.

Teacher and parent, you are the character formers, but – awful thought – the Durbeyfield ship is still at sea, and large numbers are still trapped in the hold. It is the job of the teachers to release them, but by dividing your school classes into little discussion groups you will never achieve it. You must lead them with all the guile and skill at your command.

Lead. A dirty word in this modern world. Commentators even declare leadership is not necessary in a modern day prime minister. What rubbish. History shows that all men fall into the leading or led roles, and as often as not it is the evil ones who come to the fore – the Hitlers, Stalins, Amins, and until a stronger good leader emerges, these brutes run riot, killing, maiming and cheating. The same happens in the streets of the inner towns. We read of child gangs running riot and doing endless damage, as often as not led by one boy. Is this the place they are going to occupy in a civilised society?

Civilised society. The dictionary defines civilised as:

'To make Civil, to bring out of a state of barbarism, to instruct in the arts of life, to enlighten and refine. To make proper in a civil community. To become civilised and elevated.'

Whether we like it or not, the human animal is potentially the most vicious and unpleasant creature ever bred. This streak is in all of us; so like that puppy which must be house trained, the child must be taught how to behave and conduct itself in a civilised society. Upbringing and schooling therefore have two aims, to civilise and to teach knowledge. The latter will, to a great extent, automatically follow if the first is instilled. The young must be given these qualities if they are to survive.

My wife and I recently joined a coach party for France. Our courier was in his middle fifties. Periodically throughout the trip he gave a commentary. This commentary was lucid, amusing, informative and highly professional. He was authoritative, kindly and courteous. He said he had been doing the job for eight years. I asked him what he did previously.

'Teaching.'

'Then why did you switch to this?'

'Because I could not stand it any longer.'

Oh shame. Here was a man who could lead and inform. I doubt if a single delinquent ever emerged from his care, and yet he had to give up because the teaching profession had become unbearable to him.

Democracy is a delicate plant and without careful tending, it leads to anarchy; we are on the slippery slope. Why? Because so much commonsense has departed this modern world. Please, let us have a return to commonsense.

There is something to learn from every life, and it is the duty of the older generation to pass on lessons to succeeding generations. I therefore ask myself what message I would like my grandchildren to heed if they should ever read this book. My answer is twofold: that they should practise self-reliance, (God helps those who help themselves), and that they should exercise commonsense in all things.

In this book I have shown that self-help can make tent living better, that had I not pulled myself together at KM17 I would have descended into oblivion. It is my belief that every individual must take advantage of circumstances to better himself (no, I do not mean through dishonesty), and I hope my grandchildren follow this doctrine. I quote an example of self-reliance . . .

There is a lady who lives nearby now aged ninety-four. Over recent years she has become blind, and yet she can fill a kettle from the tap, make a pot of tea and pour it without spilling a drop. I asked her how she managed it. 'By counting,' she replied. 'It takes a count of ten [say] to fill the kettle, and three to fill the cup, and there are five steps to the larder.' She has since moved into a rest home where she declines help for all but the most essential tasks. Her room is on the second floor but she refuses to use the lift for fear of pressing the emergency button and causing general panic. She therefore negotiates the most complicated stairs by herself. The result? Every member of the staff will bend over backwards to help her when she needs it. What a wonderful example she sets.

As for commonsense, do no more than listen to that marvellous gentleman who has 'Union Jacks tattooed all over his body', Sir Harvey Jones. Just about everything he expounds is based on commonsense, not sheer learning. Commonsense is an intangible product, and the older I become, the less evidence I see of it in everyday life. I hope that everything

I have written has a thread of commonsense running through it.

Scene. I am standing on Beachy Head, looking out to sea. I lower my eyes.

'Ooooh, there's a twenty pound note sitting on a tuft of thrift a few feet down the cliff.'

Commonsense tells me to leave it where it is. *Un*commonsense tells me, ' Thrift, now is the time to practise it.'

Greed despatches me downwards. I lose my grip. I land at the bottom with this and that broken. I employ the air/sea rescue service to recover my broken body. Then . . . I bring a case against Sussex County Council for not having erected a close-mesh wire fence at the top of Beachy Head to prevent twenty pound notes being blown over the edge. The judiciary, lacking the same commodity, awards damages in my favour of £250,000.

I cannot pretend that I never lacked commonsense, but I have tried. I remember my chief instructor (later Major General Tim Creasey) telling me in no uncertain terms, when I was getting 'aeriated' about a new exam marking system, to use my commonsense and shut up. I did. He was right.

What an awesome responsibility for parents and teachers. How will you measure up to your child's assessment in fifty years time? And how will my wife and I measure up to our own children's assessment? No doubt one of them will soon publish a sequel to this book entitled *So Much Hot Air!*

I started this book in the barrack room, and I take my leave from the barrack room. I have turned off the television where I have just been treated to another session of s . . . f . . . p . . . language. We are told that history repeats itself. We are in an equivalent of the Regency era, but that was sorted out by Queen Victoria who was not amused. Unfortunately no one will listen to our present day Queen if she is not amused, so will history repeat itself or not? Time will tell.

Appendix A

A LETTER FROM GERMANY IN 1905

He is very well bred and is a very capable young fellow but – to use Oxford slang – a 'rotter'. He is the typical German young man-about-town of the better class. Unlike most Germans, he speaks so quietly I can hardly tell what he says, and he generally gossips about things I am not interested in, and spoils my talk with other young men. The latter speaks English and is rather anxious to do so. He (the latter) has been in England a year and has, in consequence, a rather different view of England from what most Germans have. He rather tends to make light of the German antipathy to England whilst on the other hand the 'rotter' emphasises it strongly.

A few words on this subject of German feeling towards England. I am convinced there is an under-spread, or intense dislike, of England in Germany. It is less amongst the business and industrial class than amongst the rest. It is strongest among the 'average men', and, I imagine, in the army. It is 'Young Germany' which indulges in this sentiment. 'Young Germany' has been brought up on the tradition of the Franco-German war and the Prussian policy of making Germany a first-rate power in Europe. Hence the position of England is a perpetual thorn in the flesh to them. They are like a lot of big lads. They are sure they have the finest army in the world; they think that means everything as regards national greatness. What they want now is a big navy so as to be able to cope with

England whenever occasion shall arise. The military spirit is strong and fostered by the national institutions. Hence there is a large party ready to welcome war at any time. The fact that there is absolutely no reason why Germany should go to war except to defend her frontiers doesn't seem to strike them. They are perpetually measuring themselves, particularly against England, and there is a definite feeling that the moment England ceases to control the sea by her navy, there must be war with England.

The reason for this is simply that they are in a chronic state of jealous irritability. England has got a world empire they think, and Germany has got nothing but a few possessions in Africa. Why shouldn't Germany be on equal terms with England? For the last twenty years they have occupied themselves with theories to account for England's position. The popular view is that it is entirely due to a long policy of unscrupulous craft and cunning. They even resent the exchange of Heligoland (Salisbury's treaty of some ten years ago) as a piece of overreaching.

The most astounding piece of effrontery that I have come across is the assumption that, in regard to the Boers, they had a right to interfere on the grounds that Boers are really Germans! When I pointed out that the Boers, to say the least, are Dutch rather than German I am told it is only a question of time how long Holland will be allowed outside the Empire!

I learnt lately that the action of the English navy at the opening of the (Boer) war in forcibly examining three German vessels at South Africa to see if they were carrying ammunition to the Boers was the cause of tremendous excitement in Germany, and that a huge mob stood before the palace shouting for war to be declared against England, whilst in a respectable German magazine the sale of mules by America to England was regarded as a breach of neutrality! Chamberlain's famous 'insult to the German army' is now a fixed tradition. But what he said was perfectly and literally true and was a just, if not a wise, retort to the calumnies circulated in Germany. One idea shows how the Germans get led away by theory. They say that we have had so many men going to South Africa without any previous military training and it is these men (they think) who have perpetrated the atrocities! Anything further from the truth could hardly be imagined. Such atrocities as were committed were in the first part of the war before these volunteers arrived at the front. Moreover, the volunteers are the most respectable part of the army.

They regard the English as much more inhumane and ruthless than themselves. They have the idea too, about Ireland, that because the Irish are always clamouring for self-government, that England adopts a regular policy of oppressive cruelty. If you deny it, they appeal to the history of the sixteenth and seventeenth centuries and mention Cromwell! They forget that Cromwell has been dead for 250 years. And whilst they put up statues to Bismark in every town in Germany they ask what right have we to govern Ireland against its will.

Appendix B

A LETTER FROM THE TRENCHES, APRIL 1917

19/4/17   BEF
                                                                France

My darling Mother and Father,
You have probably seen Colonel Taing's letter by this time. What can I say to you under the circumstances?

I went over to the 2nd Btn. and got all the information I could, and from what I hear, although dear Roddie was reported missing believed killed, I am sure there is no doubt that he is dead. I understand that his Sjt, who was with him, said that he was practically dead when they put him on the stretcher, so I think that we can be quite sure he did not suffer, but died quickly like a soldier doing his duty, and as far as I can gather a credit to his regiment and father. Poor boy, it does seem such a shame. He was not twenty and yet he is now the best off of us all.

In this war, as far as I can see, the people to grieve for are not the dead, for they are finished with the whole thing. It is those that are left behind to mourn their loss that are the ones to suffer. Do not grieve for dear old Rod, it is the last thing that he himself would wish. He was a straightforward, manly, clean-hearted boy, and the Brigade staff told me that the 2nd Btn. say he did awfully well in the action, and died a hero's death; undoubtedly therefore, great will be his reward.

I must now tell you that I have given up the quartermaster work, and will join my company and go up with the Btn. in a day or so when we return to the line. Our division is going to attack again. Our battalion is leading the Brigade, and my company is leading the Btn. I am afraid we will have a rough bit of work to do, but of course, it is all the war. I will send you a postcard as soon as the show is over if I am all right, but if it should so happen that I share the fate of others, then my dear, dear parents, please accept and give my last love to all the family. We all, that is the youngsters, have had a very happy life and good time. None of us are so happy anywhere as at home. Very little sorrow of a lasting nature has touched any of us, and we have never wanted for anything that really mattered. If, as Dad has sometimes said, that cash has been a bit short, our home has always been rich in happiness and love. You, my dear father and mother, are a living example of how married life should be. I think that as a family we have been closer to each other than any family I have ever seen, and the reason of it was the example set by you to the rest of us. Therefore in the case of Roddie he had had a sheltered life, until he joined the army, where he was very happy in his regiment, and was popular with them, and he died in his full strength doing his duty like a man, a worthy son of his father, and the regiment. For him, what could be better, therefore, whether Alistair and I follow the same way as our dear brother. Always remember that if we do we shall die as men die, in full possession of our strength and faculties, and not after a long illness where death is a merciful release, and please also remember that we have had a happy life entirely through your goodness and fostering care, and that we shall die happy in the knowledge that we are serving country and proving ourselves worthy of your training and up-bringing.

And now I must stop. I hope I have not wearied you too much with this letter. You have, as you know, our deepest love and sympathy in this great trouble that has come upon us. All my thoughts are with you now.

Give my dearest love to Granny and to all the uncles and cousins, both in Ireland and in England. Give my best love to dear old Alistair when you write to him, and much to darling Mabel and Rosalind, and dear old Nigel. Poor lad, he must feel his brother's death very greatly. And with much love to you both dear Dad and Mum, and may God Almighty bless you and keep you strong through all your troubles.

I remain your loving son.

Appendix C

The Nile Delta

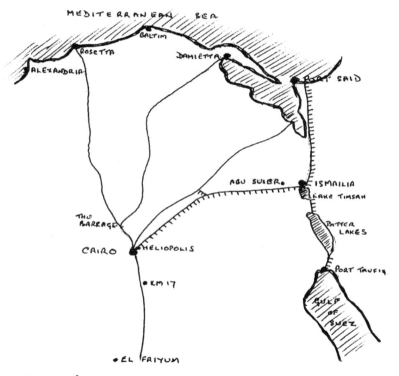

MEDITERRANEAN SEA

BALTIM

ROSETTA

DAMIETTA

ALEXANDRIA

PORT SAID

ABU SUIER

ISMAILIA

LAKE TIMSAH

THE BARRAGE

BITTER LAKES

CAIRO

HELIOPOLIS

KM 17

PORT TAUFIQ

GULF OF SUEZ

EL FAIYUM

——— R. NILE

ττττττ CANALS

NOT TO SCALE.

Appendix D

India
(Peregrinations of RHB, all visited except Rangoon)

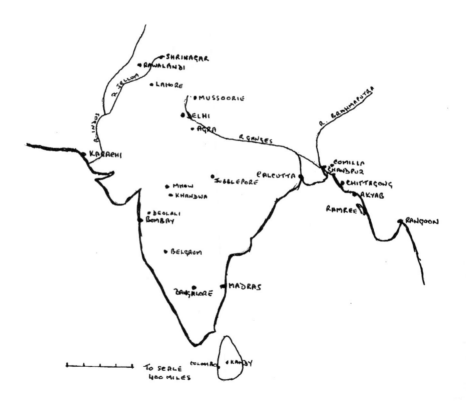

Grateful Thanks

I offer my most grateful thanks to the following:

Clayesmore, and my house master, the late JDS, for interests and values which have sustained me throughout my life;

To fellow Erks for their tolerance of an immature public school twit;

To all those men I have had the privilege to command during my commissioned service, in particular:
VV Pillai, my Indian driver and all the other IORs;
Senior NCOs, the vertebrae of my service; C/Sjt Stott, Irish Guards, Instructor at Hythe; Sjt Regan and Cpl (later Sjt) Wise in BAOR; S/Sjt Barnes at 49 Divisional Signal Regiment TA; Retired RSM Curtis, Green Howards at Inspectorate of Trade Training; and all the others, too many to list;

Signalman Sleightholme (Chapter 10, whose signature is amongst those opposite) and all the other National Servicemen who gave of their best, and against whom I will not hear a bad word;

My wife, who has patiently outlived the long and painful pregnancy of this book.

And Apologies Too

for the disappointing illustrations.

My 50 year old photographs (Abu Suier and Ramree illicit) have not reproduced well.

My sketches from photographs and memory aim to capture authenticity, not artistry.

My reasoning is that bad illustrations are better than none.

PRESENTED TO

CAPTAIN BLIZARD

FROM 10/14 HS. WRLS. GP.
BAOR 1

OCT. 30th 1950